RICK CURRY, S.J., PH.D., entered the Society of Jesus in 1961. In addition to being a Jesuit Brother for more than forty years, he's also an actor, a master baker, a teacher, and a cookbook author. He is the founder and director of the National Theatre Workshop of the Handicapped, a nonprofit acting school for persons with disabilities, which began in New York City in 1977 and has grown to include the first residential facility of the arts for persons with disabilities. Brother Curry holds a master of arts in theater from Villanova University and a doctorate in theater from New York University. He has been honored by the president of the United States with a Distinguished Service Award of the President's Committee on Employment of People with Disabilities, and has been awarded two grants from the National Endowment for the Arts. He lives in New York City and Belfast, Maine.

THE SECRETS OF
JESUIT
SOUPMAKING

A Year of Our Soups

BROTHER RICK CURRY, S.J.

PENGUIN COMPASS

PENGUIN COMPASS
Published by the Penguin Group
Penguin Putnam Inc., 375 Hudson Street,
New York, New York 10014, U.S.A.
Penguin Books Ltd, 80 Strand,
London WC2R 0RL, England
Penguin Books Australia Ltd, 250 Camberwell Road, Camberwell, Victoria 3124, Australia
Penguin Books Canada Ltd, 10 Alcorn Avenue, Toronto, Ontario, Canada M4V 3B2
Penguin Books India (P) Ltd, 11 Community Centre, Panchsheel Park, New Delhi – 110 017, India
Penguin Books (N.Z.) Ltd, Cnr Rosedale and Airborne Roads, Albany, Auckland, New Zealand
Penguin Books (South Africa) (Pty) Ltd, 24 Sturdee Avenue, Rosebank, Johannesburg 2196, South Africa

Penguin Books Ltd, Registered Offices:
Harmondsworth, Middlesex, England

First published in Penguin Compass 2002

1   3   5   7   9   10   8   6   4   2

LIBRARY OF CONGRESS CATALOGING-IN-PUBLICATION DATA
Curry, Rick, 1943–
The secrets of Jesuit soupmaking : a year of our soups / Rick Curry.
p. cm.
Includes index.
ISBN 0 14 21.9610 X
1. Soups. 2. Jesuits. I. Title.
TX757 .C87 2002
641.8'13—dc21   2002029000

PRINTED IN THE UNITED STATES OF AMERICA
Set in Perpetua
Designed by M. Paul

To my friend John Waldron Donohue, S.J.

Mentor, author, scholar, raconteur, homilist,
and faithful priest of the Society of Jesus
who continues to strengthen my gratitude for
and enthusiasm in being a Jesuit.

Contents

A Note on the Title and the Use of the Term "Ours" xi

A Note on the Stories xii

Acknowledgments xiii

Introduction 3

ADVENT

Chicken Soup 19

Clear Tomato Soup 21

Spanish Bean Soup 23

Sweet Potato Soup 26

Pot-au-Feu 28

Soupe de Compiègne 30

Cream of Corn Soup 33

Zuppa Maritata / Chicken Balls 35 / 36

Hungarian Goulash 40

Peruvian Creole Soup 42

Garlic Soup 44

Borscht 46

Cream of Fresh Tomato Soup 48

Red Bell Pepper Soup 51

Swiss Lentil, Ham, and Vegetable Soup 55

Irish Potato and Broccoli Soup 58

CHRISTMAS

Potato and Kale Soup 64

Cheddar Cheese Soup 66

Dried Corn Chowder 69

Clam and Mushroom Soup 71

Oyster Stew 72

Bongo Bongo Soup 76

Green Bean and Ham Soup 78

Chicken Leg Noodle Soup 80

Bread Dumplings 83

Matzo Balls 84

Glorified Cream of Chicken Soup 87

Mushroom-Potato Soup 90

French Cream of Mushroom Soup 94

Sherried Black Bean Soup 96

French Onion Soup 100

White Bean and Smoked Pork Soup 106

Golden Squash Soup 107

LENT

Minestrone Milanese 114

Winter Squash Soup 119

Peasant Soup 122

French Vegetable Soup 125

Mushroom and Tomato Soup 128

Bean Sprout Soup 130

Escarole Soup / Meatballs 133 / 134

CONTENTS

Dill Pickle Soup   137

Zucchini Soup   140

Chickpea and Vegetable Soup   143

Lima Bean Soup   145

Spinach Soup   150

Vichyssoise   152

Clam Chowder / Crab Chowder / Corn Chowder   157 / 158 / 159

Carrot Puree   161

EASTER

Potage aux Fines Herbes   168

Asparagus Soup   170

Potage Saint-Cloud   173

Mexican Soup   176

Avocado Soup   180

Eggplant Soup   183

Cream of Carrot Soup   185

Cream of Chicken and Apple Soup   187

Orange and Tomato Soup   190

Lobster Bisque   192

Brazilian Black Bean Soup   196

Mussel Soup Billy-Bi   198

Vegetable Soup   202

Bell Pepper Soup   204

Index   205

A Note on the Title and the Use of the Term "Ours"

DOCUMENTS FROM ROME that we read as novices always looked rather foreboding. These official communications from the "Curia" (the Jesuit headquarters in Rome) came covered in dull book jackets, and the print was ancient. You never really expected to find good news in those pages. Some of the documents were required reading, and some you had to read more than once. Stamped on the covers in large print, the Latin read *Ad Usum Nostrorum Tantum* (For the Use of Ours Only).

This use of the word "Ours" to refer to members of the Society of Jesus gradually crept into our everyday language. Instead of a Jesuit asking the question "Is he a fellow Jesuit?" he would simply inquire, "Is he one of Ours?" I love the use of "Ours" in this way, because it connotes membership—a sense of belonging—in the Brotherhood of Jesus.

When I was trying to think up a subtitle for this book about Jesuit soups, I couldn't conjure up a better one than *A Year of Our Soups,* to convey this strong sense of Jesuit identity.

A Note on the Stories

THE STORIES YOU WILL RUN ACROSS in this book are true, but I must warn you that I adhere to the Jesuit distinction between myth and truth. As John Courtney Murray, S.J., was once purported to have said, "A myth is that which never happened, but is forever true." My great friend Father Jack Alexander, S.J., told a wonderful story that absolutely delighted his audience and at the end of it a rather wet-blanket type of Jesuit came up to him and said, "Jack, I was there when that happened, and that's not exactly the way that story goes." Jack replied, "Hey, pal, you tell the story exactly the way it happened and see if you get a laugh."

This book is my attempt to capture the learning and memory that went into my soupmaking as a Jesuit brother. I hope that when you make these tangible recipes, some of Our tradition's intangibles may also reach you, for in the simplest acts, one may find the service of God.

Acknowledgments

ALL PRAYERS SHOULD BEGIN with gratitude, and in that spirit I begin this book with thanks to all who directly or indirectly helped me complete it.

Firstly, to John Spalla, dean of the National Theatre Workshop of the Handicapped who cleared all of my appointments by generously taking over my workload.

My thanks also go to Brothers Jim Horan, S.J., Jack McLane, S.J., and John Buchman, S.J., who taught me so much working alongside them in novitiate kitchens. And to John W. Donohue, S.J., of *America* magazine, who so generously read the manuscript and kept me on the straight and narrow with helpful suggestions.

Deep affection and gratitude go to my agent, Tom Colchie, who calmed several troubled waters, as well as to his lovely wife, Elaine, whose editorial help was invaluable. Lastly, special thanks go to Kevin Curtin, friend and scholar, who helped give poetry to the text, as well as to Ken Boller, S.J., and John LaRocca, S.J., who are my Jesuit cooking colleagues.

The Secrets of Jesuit Soupmaking

Introduction

Light-Up

IT'S 5:30 ON A BEAUTIFUL, crisp clear morning in October. I almost anticipate the bell, ringing to awaken us in the novitiate. The house is now particularly solemn because the first-year novices are on their long retreat of thirty days. Although this hour is usually serene, the silence seems more profound this morning. It is cold. I will not rise, shower, and prepare for the first visit as usual, because this morning I'm on light-up. I leap out of bed, kneel down, and kiss the floor, which is our humble gesture to offer our day entirely to almighty God. I get up, jump into my pants, throw on my manualia jacket—a light cotton waiter's jacket that we wear in the novitiate in lieu of our cassock—throw a towel over my shoulders while clutching my toothbrush and toothpaste, and run across the hall into the bathroom. I brush my teeth, throw water on my face, dry very quickly, and run downstairs to the kitchen.

The kitchen in the morning at Wernersville is sacred space. It is quiet as I look at all the equipment in the kitchen, which serves our men so well, awaiting like silent serpents to hiss into action. I kneel and turn on all of the spigots that activate the heat. I also turn on the oven and the top burners to begin boiling water. This is known as light-up. Looking around our kitchen, I see that the brothers from the night before have laid out much of the work, not only for breakfast, but for dinner and supper as well. Immense pots filled with bones and water sit on the stove on a low flame, making a beef stock. In another large vessel, chicken bones quietly simmer into their stock. Below the kitchen, I can hear bread pans rattling, as the brother baker puts the corn bread into the oven for breakfast. It is now time for me to look on the desk of the brother cook, and note his instructions to me for beginning the work that day.

After this duty, I slip upstairs to my room to make my hour meditation, and then join the community for Mass at eight. By the time I arrive at Mass, I feel as though I have already completed a large part of my day's work during light-up: I was the first one awake to prepare the house, to begin another day in our religious lives. Yet, in a sense, our order never sleeps, never lets the kitchen fire go wholly out—just as the Celts kept their hearths perpetually alight in ancient days. Even in the dark of night, there is a presence, a continuity of care for this kitchen that sustains us from one day to the next—a light in darkness.

Origins

IN 1994, WHILE I WAS DOING my research for *The Secrets of Jesuit Breadmaking,* I was able to go to Azpeitia in the Basque section of Spain, and to stay at Loyola Castle, which is a Jesuit community built up around the very home where Ignatius was born and raised. I spent a glorious day with a Brother Eziguera. Brother Eziguera had been a cook for many years, with a specialty in baking bread, and he spent the entire day teaching me how to make some of the most beautiful breads I'd ever seen. He taught me with gesture and silence because regrettably I speak little Spanish, and he spoke about the same amount of English. It was a joy to watch this maestro of the kitchen, and the day slipped by effortlessly. Thus, it was a surprise to discover that the evening meal had come around, and we had the perfect excuse to sup over bean soup and delicious rolls shortly before bedtime.

The following day, as I was walking down a very long corridor of Loyola Castle, a man in a cassock—a soutane—with those dark-tinted glasses the Spaniards wear, came running after me, waving his arms furiously and yelling in a rather loud voice. I didn't know what he was saying, so I quickly pulled him with me into the porter's lodge, where I knew there was a brother acting as porter who spoke English. I said to the brother, "Who *is* this person and *what* is he saying?" The Jesuit brother at the door smiled and said, "He's saying, 'Soups! Soups! What about soups? I have many recipes for your book!'" We both laughed, because we realized that he was jealous of the time that I was spending with Brother Eziguera, getting all of his marvelous bread recipes, and he was anxious to get in the book himself.

But that brother was right. It is almost impossible to separate bread from soup.

Soup is very comforting. It touches something deeply rooted in our lives. Like bread, soup is one of the earliest preparations in the recorded history of food, and doubtless predates recorded history. As soon as man possessed fire, and a fire-resistant receptacle to cook in, he began to make stews, soups, and breads. So elemental is soup that in many languages it is synonymous with, or a substitute for, the whole notion of meals or food. Expressions such as "Soup's on!" mean simply that dinner is served. The verb "to sup," meaning to eat the evening meal, and its substantive form "supper" both derive from the word "soup" or its cognate "sop," which means to dip or soak pieces of food—of course, usually bread—in broth, wine, or some other liquid.

When I first left home for the Jesuits and entered the novitiate at Wernersville, Pennsylvania, I was surprised to find that soup was such a major part of the Jesuit diet. Soup was served during the noontime meal and again at the main meal at six o'clock. My first job as a novice brother was in the kitchen, and I was amazed to find that there were always several pots of soup in the making. It was a work in progress. There would be a soup cooking for the noon meal. The evening soup was often the noon meal revisited, with some vegetables or other ingredients added. Perhaps a pot of beginning soup simmered away that we would serve three days hence. Another large stockpot sat bubbling, filled with bones and water to create a meat stock or a brown stock. And maybe another pot cooked along, filled with vegetables, water, and seasonings to make a vegetable stock. It was often difficult for me even to predict which soup would be served at the meal when I went out to the dining room, because I would forget exactly which soup was on for that day. But whatever soup was served, it always arrived at table to great welcome. And sitting down at the refectory table after a tough morning, or a rigorous afternoon—laughing, saying grace, listening to the reading, then sitting in silence—it was always a delight to dip the spoon deep, and nourish ourselves with a comforting bowl of soup. Hot and hearty, soup warmed and cheered us during those cold Wernersville winters, and gave me the courage to go on in my early days of introduction to Jesuit life.

In those days, the early sixties before Vatican II, the kitchen and indeed all cooking was the domain of the Jesuit brother. Nowadays, many of our priests and practically all our scholastics (those Jesuits preparing to become priests) cook for each other. My good friend Father Ken Boller, S.J., pastor of St. Aloysius in Harlem, regularly cooks for his small community, and gets rave reviews for his food. But in the pre–Vatican II era, the brother who had a reputation as a good cook reigned supreme. He was greatly loved, and given the credit for nourishing, literally and figuratively, many Jesuit vocations.

As novice brothers, we all aspired to be greatly admired, and the shortcut to fame and adulation was to learn to cook well. This human ambition was tempered by the formal training we were receiving as "baby Jesuits." In our conferences, institute classes, daily exhortations, spiritual reading, Scripture classes, and personal spiritual direction, we were learning about the vision St. Ignatius had for his followers.

Ignatius believed that the simplest of human activities should be done for God's greater glory by serving one another. Therefore, we were to become good cooks to better serve God's people, and this lesson could be learned by observing the quiet example of those great brothers who were charged with teaching us the rudimentary skills of cooking.

It might look to some in those pre–Vatican II days that our lives during our early days of training were rather monastic. Indeed, they were formal, but Ignatius Loyola's concept of a religious order represents a break with the monastic tradition of religious life. Whereas the monastic orders traditionally gathered their members as a community to serve God by prayer, liturgy, study, and manual work in the monastery, Ignatius envisioned an order of men able to respond to needs in any part of the world; living in the diaspora for the sake of apostolic service.

Ignatius's break with the monastic tradition is also evident in the kind and amount of prayer he felt was appropriate for Jesuits. The Jesuit vocation is undoubtedly a contemplative vocation, but in a rather specialized sense: for while it is "in action" that we are called to be contemplative, this cannot obscure the fact that we are called to be contemplative. The underlying idea here is that a person called to be "contemplative in the midst of daily life" might better feel the desire to pray on a more real and consistent basis.

It is this spirituality in the midst of daily life that I find so appealing about St. Ignatius Loyola. It took a long time for this saint to grow on me. Ignatius is a slow take. He certainly doesn't have the appeal of a St. Francis of Assisi, or even a Mother Teresa. Why is this great mystic, great founder, and educator so elusive? Early on, I was afraid of him. As a novice, and even as a young brother in studies, I was determined to be the perfect religious and observe every rule to the letter. This feeling of rigidity was reinforced by all those statues of St. Ignatius—pointing with one hand to the rule book that he carried in his other hand. It took years to discover that there was freedom in those rules and constitutions. It also took years to discover that Ignatius as a personality leads you to *Christ,* not to himself.

But what I found most appealing about St. Ignatius Loyola was his insight that you could find God in all things. If you followed Ignatius's teachings, then you could certainly find God in soups—not only in the soups themselves, but also in the service that went into the soups. Moreover, not just the service that went into the soups, but how we made the soups themselves—our entire way of proceeding. When you enter the Society of Jesus, you're introduced to a 450-year-old tradition: you're indoctrinated into our way of life, our methodology, and then you are taught the very specific skills that are needed in day-to-day activities. But always over and above the daily activities there is a much greater reason for doing the simplest acts, and that is *ad majorem Dei gloriam:* for the great honor and glory of God.

It was clear from the very establishment of the Jesuits that Ignatius wanted you to be good at what you did. He certainly wanted people who cook to be excellent cooks. Father Jeronimo Nadal (1507–1560), an early Jesuit, put this attitude clearly in an exhortation at Alcalá when he said, "The Society wants men who are as accomplished as possible in every discipline that helps it in its purpose. Do not be satisfied with doing it halfway."

I learned how to cook the same way I learned how to pray—through practice. Certainly, a Jesuit is mandated to pray daily, as are all Christians. I decided to learn how to cook in as systemized a way as I approached my prayer life. I also decided that I would try to cook every day. Even in communities where I was not assigned as the cook, I often prepared food for the community on weekends.

WHEN I WAS FIRST ASSIGNED to the kitchen in the novitiate, I really didn't think that I would be able to accomplish anything besides washing the pots and pans. The beautiful things that came out of the oven looked wondrous, and to me out of reach. I never thought that I would be able to cook like that. But as time went on and I became more confident in my skills in the kitchen, and the brother cook became more confident in my abilities, he let me dive in to do the job. The older brothers let me know that what we were talking about here was some water, some vegetables, and some heat: just go and do it, and learn by doing it under their watchful eyes, then do it again. Repetition is a key concept of Jesuit pedagogy that's very much overlooked today. The Jesuits believe that one best learns by repeating something over and over and over again; and the *Ratio Studiorum*—the Jesuit code of methodology and curriculum—recommends *repetitio* as a very definite form of learning. At the novitiate in Wernersville, we made very many different kinds of soup on a weekly basis. I cooked those soups over and over and over again, learning more about them each time I repeated the process.

A Place to Work—A Place to Pray

THE NOVITIATE IS REALLY MORE than just a house, or even a locale. And the kitchen, particularly in the novitiate, is really more than just a kitchen. A kitchen in a novitiate is a place where people take care of people, and in so doing express something intangible—something about life, love, service, and caring—through the cooking itself. It is about serving God in all things. It is about the simple act of cooking in the service of almighty God. But among the tangibles that we're best known for in the kitchen are the wonderful soups that come out of it. Oh, there were days, of course, when soup involved just opening a can and adding some water or some milk. But there were other soups—soups that we labored over, soups that we spent time with, soups that we were able to create stocks for—and these soups are the ones that I want to talk about.

Ignatius's advice on the approach to prayer was to find space, give time, make it your time, enjoy it, and reflect upon it. The first thing that I do when I begin to work is take a deep breath, place myself in the presence of God, and let Him know that I know that I'm engaged in a wonderful, sacred activity. This is my own personal time, and this is my own personal space, and this is something that I enjoy. I'm participating in a life-giving and pleasure-giving product.

When Ignatius taught the Jesuits to pray, he insisted that they be comfortable. They could pray sitting, lying down, standing, kneeling, or in any other position where they were at ease. Obviously, you can take this approach in your kitchen and make yourself comfortable while you cook soup. You can create an environment in which you feel relaxed and enjoy the process. You should feel good as you make something good.

You don't need a dream kitchen to make a great pot of soup. Find some free counter space, or a table on which you can put all your ingredients and still have some room to mix them together and to throw some vegetables around. For me, free counter space means clearing away all the obstacles on it. When I was at Xavier University in Cincinnati in 1965 I took a creative writing course with Mr. Feldhouse, an extraordinary teacher of writing, who said, "Don't encumber yourself with small pieces of paper. Get large pieces of paper and write all over them and *clear off* your desk."

I say, *clear off* your work space!

I also urge you to pay attention to the height of your counter or table. Find the best height for your use. Working at one that is too high or too low can put stress on your back, and turn an enjoyable activity into a painful one. I'm over six feet tall, and my good friend Kirk Moore built me a butcher-block table forty-eight inches high, the perfect height for me. He finds it a bit excessive when I say that this gift has changed my life, but if you've ever struggled with lower back pain, you'll agree this claim is only a slight exaggeration. I also have a small step stool handy, should I need more height and leverage over the ingredients. If you're stuck with a counter that is too high for you, raise yourself by standing on a step stool or even on a phone book. Or if your counter is too low, do your slicing and dicing on a board that has been raised by a phone book.

Tools

In the novitiate, we learned to respect our tools. The brothers taught us that they had to last, so they must be taken care of. We were taught to clean our utensils as we used them—we couldn't let them accumulate in the sink. At the end of a long day of cooking, all those pots and utensils piled up waiting to be scrubbed and washed would have been quite a daunting sight. So we cleaned as we went. We washed the utensils the minute we were finished with them.

In those early days in the Jesuit kitchen, I was always amazed to see what wonderful food the brothers were able to produce with such simple tools. In fact, I think that there is a correlation. I absolutely believe in keeping all the utensils simple. Too much sophisticated machinery (although I do appreciate the food processor) can detract from the basics of good cooking. Clearly, you need a good knife, a pot, a bowl, a spoon, some measuring cups, and a stove, but also, most important, a little peace and quiet.

For stocks, a large, heavy stockpot is essential, because a quantity of bones tends to take up a lot of room. Beef broth needs a kettle that holds at least twelve quarts, but chicken broth can be prepared in a ten-quart pot. Three-quart saucepans are also needed for first-course soups, and remember that as a rule of thumb, a heavier pan heats more evenly, but it should not be so heavy that it's hard to handle. For the full-meal soups, a versatile five- to six-quart Dutch oven or a deep kettle can be very helpful. For many stews, you can make use of a deep ten- to twelve-inch frying pan. To strain out the bones and vegetables in homemade broth, you need a large colander with fine perforations; and for turning cooked vegetable mixtures into creamy purees, you'll need a blender or food processor. Both do the job superbly, but the food processor offers the additional convenience of grating, shredding, slicing, and chopping vegetables and other soup ingredients. You also can use that old standby, a hand-operated food mill, to puree vegetables, which we used in the novitiate long before food processors were on the market.

THIS BOOK IS ORGANIZED according to the major seasons of the Catholic liturgical year, as was my earlier one on bread. Thus, Advent and Christmas seasons will tend to feature wintery soups, often with meat. Lent and Easter feature lighter, clearer vegetarian soups. However, many of the winter soups work fine during the Lenten fasting days, if you just omit the meat and use vegetable stock. In passing, I suggest some breads that go best with these soups as well, since bread and soup have always been considered a marriage made in heaven. I have also included some dumpling and meatball recipes.

Stock

MANY PEOPLE FEEL that they don't have time to make soup from scratch. But you really don't need to devote nine or ten hours to making soup, or even three or four hours. You work on the soup for ten minutes, and then you let it go for an hour and a half or two hours, or four hours. You come back to work on it for fifteen minutes longer, and then just put it on top of your stove and let it simmer. I like to think of making soup as an ongoing relationship, because soup is a living thing, and like other living things, it can, in fact, be left alone at times to grow and become something of itself on its own.

At the heart of this process is the creation of various stocks. Stock recipes are simply building blocks for making truly great and tasty soups. Stock is the liquid extracted by cooking the bones of meat, fowl, or fish in a big pot over a slow, low heat. This liquid is concentrated flavor to make your soups delicious. It's your chance to be creative and not feel hemmed in by stringent rules or measures. Stock-making is not an exact science nor should it be. To guarantee success, tip the scales in your favor by making sure that all the stuff that goes into your stock is fresh and flavorful.

Making stock involves the slow drawing out of essential flavors, spices, and nutrients from both vegetable and animal sources, using the medium of cold, pure water. The cook slowly brings the water up to the room temperature of the ingredients, which can then be thrown in. The mixture is then slowly heated until the surface water in the stockpot settles into the gentlest possible simmer. Soup is a "back burner" food, and some of the better cooking-supply stores offer burner covers that can blunt the heat of the typical burner—perfect for making delicate sauces or soup. Meat stocks like beef and chicken benefit from long, slow simmering, because it takes longer to draw the flavors out of the bones, the marrow, and the flesh and connective tissue. A vegetable stock—and there are many varieties possible—does not benefit from an overly long cooking time. When you've drawn out the essential flavors in a couple of hours, that's it. It is best to stop the process then. Of course, a good cook always tastes periodically to determine this stopping point. Meat stocks tend to require more skimming of the fats and foams that float to the top.

Chicken Stock

Now, there are endless discussions among soup cooks about the proper "age or maturity" of ingredients to make soup. A little common sense here helps. Remember that the origin of soup arose from early cooks with scarce resources. They made the most of what spare vegetables and meat they could find. Of course in lean times you would grab that old hen who could no longer lay eggs for the family, or the muscular but now elderly rooster, to anchor your broth. The old Italian saw goes *Gallina vecchia fa buon brodo* (An old chicken makes good broth). Yet, this is really making a virtue of necessity. How many of us have access to aged chickens? Anyone who cooks with chicken knows one thing: organic free-range chicken is to the overprocessed commercial fowl as pheasant is to tofu. They are two different things entirely. Cook a free-range organic chicken, and the juices and pan drippings run darker, the meat is also darker; and more flavorful. Supermarket chickens are quite bland when you get right down to it, and that is why cooks have to tart them up with extra seasonings, marinades, and sauces. Doesn't it make sense that a healthy organic free-range chicken can make a superior soup? So forget old dead birds. Good chicken makes good soup; as do vegetables that you would really like to eat, instead of stuff best thrown away on the compost pile. You are only as good as your ingredients in the cooking game. Yet . . . if you want to make like Marie Antoinette out in the rear of the castle raising, distressing, and aging scrawny roosters, knock yourself out.

But, truly, if you want to try cooking soup with one kind of chicken, then switch off with another to compare, you will walk away a better soup cook. You cook better soup through the pure experience of the craft—tasting, adjusting seasonings, refining quantity and quality of ingredients. This is cooking.

There are different ways of beginning a stock. Some people throw in the aromatics—leeks, garlic, onions, celery and celery leaves—along with the chicken and water. I like to lightly sauté, or "sweat," the onions and garlic in a little olive oil, because the flavors open up a lot more. Further, oil absorbs and carries the seasonings and essences of this soffritto throughout the broth. It is a small step, but one that really makes a difference in all cooking. Cheesecloth bags of selected herbs also add a depth to the developing stock.

A couple of final points: There is no law that says that you can't remove the meat from the chicken breast midway through the cooking process. This way, it doesn't cook into stringy toughness, and you can cut it up into juicy bite-size pieces for the final chicken soup. Some people specially season this chicken breast to reintroduce into the final broth, imparting more pizzazz to things.

When the stock is ready, you can strain it through cheesecloth, and you can wet this with cold water to catch more fat and impurities. There is nothing wrong with lightly pressing all the solids as you strain, to catch more of the stock's essences. You can further clarify a stock by refrigerating overnight, then skimming off the top layer just before you begin to reheat it. (The fatty layer acts to seal in flavor in the refrigerator.) This gives you units of stock that you can incorporate into many recipes.

If you finish your chicken soup with an addition of orzo, or other pasta shapes, be sure to cook it independently until al dente—"toothsome," in Italian—so that it stands up well over time in the broth.

BEEF STOCK

A simple beef broth can be generated with:

3 pounds rump roast, butt portion
1 onion, halved
1 clove garlic, peeled and crushed
2 celery ribs
1 large carrot, roughly chopped
1 fresh tomato or 1 small canned tomato

Put all the ingredients into a stockpot, and cover with 3 inches of water. Simmer and skim from time to time for 3½ to 4 hours. Strain through cheesecloth. Cool, then refrigerate.

MEAT STOCK

To make about five pints of meat stock begin by throwing into the pot a 7- or 8-pound heap of meaty bones and meat. It doesn't matter that these meats are of different types. To this add some chicken necks, giblets, and even whole chicken carcasses. Next come the vegetables, including 1 large unpeeled onion, and 2 celery stalks cut into large pieces. When they're available, I throw in two leeks cut into large pieces. If you have any parsnips around, cut one or two and toss them in. For a little zest I often add 4 to 6 unpeeled garlic cloves, which I crush lightly before adding to the pot. For first-class feasts, I'll throw in some cloves to mark the special occasion. The last touch is the bouquet garni, which is a bundle of spices or herbs that are tied together in a cheesecloth bag and tied onto the handle of the stockpot so that they can be removed easily when the cooking is completed. My regular ingredients for the bouquet garni bag include celery leaves, bay leaves, and thyme sprigs, all tied together.

I squish and press the vegetables around the meat and bones and add cold water to about two inches above the mass of ingredients in the pot. Light a fire under it and bring it to a boil, skimming foam off the surface with a slotted spoon as it appears. When the stock reaches the boiling point I reduce the heat and add the bouquet garni and simmer slowly in an uncovered pot for about five hours. During that time I go about my other duties, returning regularly to skim off the surface and check on the progress.

After five hours I line a strainer with damp cheesecloth and ladle the liquid from the stockpot into the strainer. Refrigerate after it's been ladled off.

BROWN STOCK

To make a brown stock just put the bones and the meat and vegetables in a large pan and brown the ingredients in a preheated 450-degree oven for a half an hour, turning occasionally. Finally, put all this in a stockpot, discarding the fat. Proceed as you would with the meat stock.

VEGETABLE STOCK

As stated above, you build up a vegetable stock from onions, scallions, fresh ginger, leeks, garlic—sautéing them in olive oil until the aromatics wilt and open up their flavor. A crushed peppercorn in the soffritto doesn't hurt, but pepper and garlic are not for all times or all soups. Celery, and especially the leaves from good stalks, will impart a lot of flavor, as will parsley, carrots, diced zucchini, green beans, cabbage, kale, Swiss chard, pumpkin, potatoes, and tomatoes. Many recipes call for dicing your vegetables into uniform size. Vegetable stocks are really wide open to experimentation. You can add a wonderful element to any of these stocks by throwing a handful of roughly torn basil into the finished broth. You can make a potato soup base merely by simmering diced potatoes, leeks, water, and onions. This can be really luxurious if you first sauté good mushrooms in olive oil or butter for a good while, then add the other ingredients for a slow simmer.

Advent

Take, oh Lord, and receive all my liberty,

my memory, my understanding, and my entire

will. Whatever I have or hold, you have given

me; I restore it all to you and surrender it

wholly to be governed by your will. Give me

only your love and your grace, and I am rich

enough and ask for nothing more.

ST. IGNATIUS LOYOLA

As Psalm 25 says, "Guide me in your truth and teach me, for you are God my Savior. For you I wait all the long day, because of your goodness, Lord." Waiting is an essential part of spiritual life, but waiting as a disciple of Jesus is not an empty wait. It's a waiting with a promise in our hearts, making already present that for which we are waiting. We wait during Advent for the birth of Jesus. I often think that the long years of preparation for final vows, or to be ordained a Jesuit priest, is that sense of Advent. But ask any Jesuit who has gone through those years of training, and we will tell you we never felt that we were just treading water, or biding time. Each day is so rich and full in the service of the Lord that we are actually in an act of becoming. Not becoming full-fledged Jesuits overnight through a predictable ordination or final vows, we're becoming more like disciples, waiting for God with an active, alert, and joyful attitude. As we wait, we remember Him for whom we are waiting, and as we remember Him, we create a community prepared to welcome Him when He comes. This great sense of Advent is what always prepared us for the joyful coming of the Incarnation. How do we wait for God? We wait with patience. But patience doesn't mean passivity. Waiting patiently is really not like waiting for a bus or for rain to stop, it's an active waiting, in which we live the present moment to the full in order to find those signs of our love for God for which we are waiting.

I am reminded of a young Jesuit whose mother came to visit him in New York City. Prior to her visit, he got a call from his aunt, who said, "I'm wondering if you have some time to sit down with your mother and talk with her. I live with your mother, and her lack of patience is driving us all crazy." The young Jesuit said that he would try. Well into her visit, the time seemed right, and he said to his mother, "Mom, I would really like to talk to you about your patience." "Oh, dear," she replied. "I don't have any left. I used to have a little left, but your sister took that. Now it's all gone."

I love that story because I can relate to it so well. It's as if we think of patience as a jar of tomato sauce on a shelf, and when we use it up, there isn't any more. But that's not true. The word "patience" comes from the Latin verb *patior*, which means "to suffer." Waiting patiently means to suffer through the present moment. But it's tasting it to the full, and letting the seeds that are sown in the ground on which we stand grow into a strong plant. Waiting patiently also means paying attention to what is happening right before our eyes, and seeing the first rays of God's glory coming. This is Advent. Our life is a perpetual Advent, waiting for the full coming in our lives of the Lord Jesus. When we have the Lord to look forward to, we can already experience him in the waiting. Psalm 27 says, "Wait for the Lord, take courage, be stouthearted, wait for the Lord."

SOUP IS COMFORTING, because our palates have memories, and soup can remind us of the security we felt around the family table in childhood. What we experience are memories of love. If soups are comforting, then no soup is more comforting than chicken soup. Its healing properties are legendary, and I suspect that there may be scientific proof that chicken soup is penicillin for the soul. Real health comes from strong memories of love, and chicken soup holds this healing power for me.

The making of chicken soup appears simple, but it is not. It requires attention to detail, and the secret is a great chicken. A fowl hen, or stewing chicken, is my favorite. Best of all possible worlds is a hen that has been organically raised, and that has been free to range and grow. Naturally, it should be as fresh as possible. Approximately 6 pounds is the appropriate size for a fowl, which can be cooked in 3 quarts of water to provide generous amounts of rich soup.

The pot is not insignificant. Ideally, it should be taller than it is wide, and relatively narrow, with straight sides, as that shape enables the most efficient use of water. Pots with aluminum cooking surfaces are best avoided.

Chicken Soup

1 (6-pound) fowl or 8 pounds broilers, with neck and all giblets
    except liver
2 medium carrots, scraped and quartered
2 to 3 celery ribs, with leaves, whole or cut in half
1 medium yellow onion, whole or cut in half, peeled or unpeeled
3 parsley sprigs
8 to 10 black peppercorns
2 to 3 teaspoons coarse salt or 1 to 2 teaspoons table salt to taste

SINGE THE CHICKEN as close to cooking time as possible, so as to lose little of the fat. Quarter the chicken into manageable pieces, and place these into a 5-quart pot. A whole chicken should fit easily into a pot of 6 or 7 quarts.

Add water to cover the chicken. Bring to a boil, and then reduce the heat to a slow simmer. Foam should rise during this process; simply skim it off the top. Once the foam subsides, add the carrots, celery, onion, parsley, peppercorns, and 1 teaspoon salt.

Cook the mixture until the chicken falls off the bones. Broilers should be cooked for 1¼ hours, fowl for 2 or 3 hours. Allow 15 extra minutes for whole broilers, 30 minutes for whole fowl. If the water should fall below seven-eighths of the pot height, refill until the chicken is covered. Turn two or three times while the soup cooks, tasting and adding salt as needed.

Remove the chicken, giblets, and bones, and set all aside. Pour the soup through a sieve, rinse the pot, and if the soup is to be served immediately, return it to the pot.

SERVES: 6 TO 8

I'VE ALWAYS ASSOCIATED Clear Tomato Soup with St. Robert Bellarmine (1542–1621), whose Feast Day is September 17. On September 17, 1961, I left home to begin my religious life at the Jesuit novitiate of St. Isaac Jogues in Wernersville, Pennsylvania. It was a Sunday. I arrived at around 1:30, and by six o'clock I was seated in a massive refectory, listening to the life of St. Robert Bellarmine. My memory of him was as a Jesuit, a cardinal, and a holy man, and this was followed by tomato soup. I also remember his fear of becoming pope, and his prayer, "From the papacy, deliver me, oh Lord!"

Clear Tomato Soup

1 tablespoon butter

1 tablespoon olive oil

1 large onion, chopped

2 tablespoons flour

4 cups water

6 chicken bouillon cubes

1 large rib celery, with leaves, chopped

1 (28-ounce) can tomatoes, with their liquid

2 teaspoons sugar

1 teaspoon dried basil

1 bay leaf

Juice of 1 small lemon or lime, strained

1 tablespoon Worcestershire sauce

Few drops of Tabasco sauce

Salt to taste

Croutons or finely chopped parsley, for garnish

HEAT THE BUTTER and oil in a large saucepan and cook the onion until translucent. Stir in the flour and cook the mixture over gentle heat for a few minutes. Gradually add the water, stirring until the mixture is slightly thickened and smooth. Add the bouillon cubes, celery, tomatoes, sugar, basil, and bay leaf.

Bring the mixture to a boil, reduce the heat, and simmer, covered, for 30 minutes. Strain the soup and discard the residue.

Season with the lemon juice and Worcestershire sauce along with the Tabasco sauce and salt to taste. Serve hot, garnished with croutons, or chilled, garnished with parsley.

SERVES: 6

THE MEMORY OF ST. FRANCIS BORGIA is recalled on his feast day, October 3. He was the third superior general of the Society of Jesus, and the first to send missionaries to Florida, the earliest mission in America. Borgia was the eldest son of the Duke of Gandia, and became duke himself after his father's death. Francis married and, with his wife and eight children, had a close relationship with the emperor Charles V and his wife, Isabella. Charles's wife died unexpectedly at the age of thirty-six. Prior to her interment, the coffin was opened. According to a legendary story, when Borgia looked at Isabella, he saw to his surprise that her face was decomposing. Borgia vowed, "Never more will I serve a master who can die." In 1546, he became acquainted with the Jesuits, especially Father Peter Faber, one of the original members. Francis founded a Jesuit college in Gandia, which impressed Father Faber so much that he alerted Ignatius to Borgia's resolve to enter the Society. Ignatius accepted him secretly. Borgia continued to live as duke until he pronounced his vows in 1550, and earned a doctorate in theology from the very college he founded. Eventually, he went to live with Ignatius in Rome. Afterward, he left for Spain, resigned his title, and donned the Jesuit cassock. St. Francis Borgia was ordained on May 23, 1551, and in 1564 became superior general, a position he held for only seven years before Pope Pius V asked him to oversee building Gesù Church in Rome.

Spanish Bean Soup is a dish worthy of his memory.

Spanish Bean Soup

2 ½ cups dried small white beans, rinsed and drained (about 1
    pound)
2 teaspoons salt
6 cups water
2 smoked ham hocks (about 1 ½ pounds)
1 large onion, finely chopped
2 ribs celery, with leaves, finely chopped
1 large clove garlic, minced or pressed
2 medium potatoes, diced
2 small turnips, peeled and diced
4 small chorizo sausages (about ¾ pound)
1 bunch of spinach (about 12 ounces)
Salt to taste
Cilantro (Chinese parsley), for garnish

PLACE THE BEANS IN A LARGE BOWL; add 2 teaspoons
salt and 6 cups water. Cover and let stand for at least 8 hours; drain,
discarding soaking liquid. Or to shorten the soaking period, place
beans in a 3- to 4-quart pan with 8 cups of water (no salt). Bring to a
boil; then boil briskly, uncovered, for 2 minutes. Remove from heat,
cover, and let stand for about 1 hour. Drain and discard the soaking
liquid.

In a 5- to 6-quart kettle, combine the drained beans, the 6
cups water, ham hocks, onion, celery, garlic, potatoes, and turnips.
Bring to a boil over medium heat. Cover, reduce heat, and boil gently
until beans are very tender (3 ½ to 4 hours).

Meanwhile, remove and discard sausage casings and slice
sausages ½ inch thick. In a medium frying pan over moderate heat,
cook the sausages in their own drippings, stirring often, until lightly

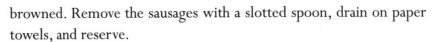

browned. Remove the sausages with a slotted spoon, drain on paper towels, and reserve.

Remove the ham hocks from the beans. When they are cool enough to handle, discard bones and skin; cut the ham into large chunks and return to the soup. Add the prepared sausage; then cook, uncovered, stirring occasionally, for about 10 minutes.

Meanwhile, rinse and drain the spinach. Remove and discard the stems. Coarsely shred the leaves; add to the soup and cook, stirring, until spinach is just wilted and bright green. Taste, and add salt if needed.

Serve the hot soup garnished with sprigs of cilantro.

SERVES: 6 TO 8

"I'M COMING, LORD" was the greeting every visitor heard at the Jesuit College of Montesion in Palma, on the island of Majorca. It was the greeting offered by Brother Alphonsus Rodriguez, the first Jesuit brother to be canonized. His father was a wool merchant in Segovia, and Alphonsus carried on his father's business, married, and had three children. In rapid succession, his wife and children succumbed to illness and died. His business failed soon afterward, on account of heavy taxation. During this period of mourning, he devoted himself totally to the Lord. After several years, Rodriguez applied to the Society of Jesus, and was refused. He applied again, and was again refused because of his age and poor health. But the provincial overrode this decision. Blessed Peter Faber, one of the first companions of St. Ignatius, knew Alphonsus as a little boy and is supposed to have said that while Rodriguez might not be qualified to be a priest, he could enter the Society as a brother to become a saint. Alphonsus was thirty-seven when he began his novitiate. For the next forty-six years, he faithfully served as a brother and porter. He became an astute spiritual director, and later advised young Peter Claver, urging him to volunteer for the South American missions. Peter followed his advice, and went to Cartagena, Colombia, where he labored among the slaves and earned his own sainthood. When Brother Alphonsus died on October 31, 1617, the townspeople demanded that he be given a public burial, and immediately revered him as a saint. We often had combination St. Alphonsus Rodriguez / Halloween parties, and later I served Sweet Potato Soup on these occasions.

Sweet Potato Soup

2 ribs celery, trimmed and chopped

2 medium onions, chopped

3 medium sweet potatoes, peeled and chopped

4 cups water

4 beef bouillon cubes

1 bay leaf

1½ teaspoons dried tarragon

2 cups milk, scalded

Salt to taste

White pepper to taste

Chopped parsley, for garnish

COMBINE THE CELERY, onions, sweet potatoes, water, bouillon cubes, bay leaf, and tarragon in a large saucepan. Bring to a boil, reduce the heat, and simmer, covered, for about 30 minutes, until the sweet potatoes are very tender. Whirl the mixture in a food processor, 2 cupfuls at a time, until it is smooth. Add the puree and the scalded milk to the saucepan. Bring the soup to serving temperature. Season to taste with salt and pepper. Add parsley, for garnish.

SERVES: 6 TO 8

ALTHOUGH BEING THE BROTHER COOK looks like a humble job, it is, in fact, a very powerful one. The army of Christ travels on its stomach like any other. The brothers were clever in announcing their influential stewardship, even in subtle ways. Every subculture has its own language, and the brothers, a minority in the Society of Jesus, are no different from other minorities. The first evidence of this was on the feast of the North American martyrs, commemorating St. Isaac Jogues and six others in the society who were martyred in the 1640s. But the brothers showed this subtlety by making a special fuss over St. René Goupil, a Jesuit brother who was killed while at prayer, in particular for having made the sign of the cross over an Indian child. He is remembered by a shrine near the place of his death, in Auriesville, New York. How did we commemorate him? Pot-au-feu.

Pot-au-Feu

1 pound beef short ribs

3 to 4 pounds bottom round or chuck

1 pound beef soup bones

1 large onion, stuck with 3 cloves

1 clove garlic

6 to 8 whole peppercorns

2 tablespoons salt

1 bunch of parsley, finely chopped

3 sprigs of dill

1 bunch of celery, including leaves

3 bay leaves

½ teaspoon dried thyme

12 carrots, peeled

2 turnips, peeled

2 parsley roots (if available), peeled

2 to 3 leeks, cleaned

2 pounds marrowbones, washed

1 cup fresh or frozen peas

PUT ALL THE MEAT and soup bones in a large kettle. Cover with water. Add the onion, garlic, peppercorns, salt, chopped parsley, dill, celery leaves, bay leaves, and thyme. Bring all to a boil, then reduce flame.

Cover and simmer for 1½ hours, skimming the foam off the top with a slotted spoon. Add all the remaining vegetables (except for the peas) and the marrowbones. Cook for 20 minutes, then add the peas and continue to cook for 5 more minutes.

SERVES: 8 TO 10

MY PARENTS WERE BETWEEN HOUSES, and it was more convenient to have me invite them to Thanksgiving dinner at our small community at St. Joseph's University than to have them set up a makeshift eatery. The guest list included my parents, as well as Father Henry Lavin, S.J., and his mother, and myself. Of course, I wanted the meal to be perfect and reflect the wonderful Thanksgiving dinner my mother had always prepared so lovingly. However, what seemed effortless for my mother was exhausting for me. "How did Mom do this?" I kept asking myself all day.

I cooked the turkey, and searched my memory for the dressing and the rest of my family's favorite vegetables. I even baked two pies—one mincemeat and one pumpkin. My guests judged the feast a huge success up until the dessert. When I announced the choices for dessert, Mrs. Lavin replied that only ice cream constituted dessert in her book. Unfortunately, my ice cream larder was bare, and the rest of us ate our pie in relative silence, supressing our laughter. All of us, though, enjoyed this Soupe de Compiègne, which was the first course that day.

Soupe de Compiègne

1 ½ cups diced onions
⅛ teaspoon sugar
4 tablespoons butter
½ teaspoon dry mustard
3 cups lamb stock
1 cup milk
1 egg yolk, beaten
½ cup heavy cream
Salt to taste
Cayenne pepper to taste
Slivered pimiento
Minced fresh parsley and/or chives, for garnish

SPRINKLE THE ONIONS with the sugar and sauté them in the butter until they begin to turn golden. Sprinkle with the mustard and cook for 2 minutes. Add the stock and then cover, bringing to a boil. Lower the heat and simmer until the onions are soft.

Puree the onions, then add the milk, and reheat. Whisk the egg yolk and cream with ½ cup of hot soup, and add this to the rest of the soup. Reheat, but do not boil.

Adjust with salt and cayenne pepper to taste and garnish with pimiento and parsley.

SERVES: 4 TO 6

THANKSGIVING AT WERNERSVILLE was for most of us our first major feast away from home. Mothers are so much at the heart of family feasts that it seemed disheartening to have this holiday without our loved ones. And, of course, everyone had his favorite dish at Thanksgiving, which only his mother could produce. It was a daunting task for the brother cook to create a meal that could compete with memories of Mom and home.

The day was highlighted by the Jogues Bowl, a touch football game between the novices and the juniors named after St. Isaac Jogues (1607–1646), the North American martyr and patron of our novitiate. We brought a white heat of energy and enthusiasm to this spectacle. An elderly and witty father likened the novices' gridiron zeal to the wild zest the Mohawks displayed in torturing and tomahawking our martyr St. Isaac Jogues. It was a battle royal, with athletic egos on the line; and at times it was hard to remember that we were in training to be men for others, and not wild braves glorying in the sack of their opponents.

During my era, the novices always won, and so we entered the refectory flush with victory, and a bit more heartened to face Thanksgiving without our families. What a feast awaited us. Each table had a beautiful plump turkey in the center, with all the trimmings—soon filling us all to bursting. However, there was a strange-looking bowl of sauerkraut on each table, and the brothers let us know that it was a Jesuit culinary tradition to have our meals reflect the particular culture in which we were residing. Wernersville was in Pennsylvania Dutch territory, and its people reveled in sweet-and-sour. If you had sweet cranberry sauce, then the sauerkraut would provide the sour. What a great and early lesson in acculturation.

Throughout our history, the Jesuit brothers went ahead of the fathers to foreign lands to learn the customs of the people as well as the language. By the time the priests arrived, the brothers were able to act as translators, and had prepared the housing and the food for the new Jesuit community. Therefore, a new mission always hit the road running. The brothers learned much from the native peoples, and in some cases, these European brothers were able to provide valuable agricultural techniques for the local farmers to increase their crop yields. Here's a soup that the Native Americans and the Pennsylvania Dutch can both agree on.

Cream of Corn Soup

3 tablespoons butter

1 large onion, chopped

4 tablespoons flour

3 cups water

4 chicken bouillon cubes, crushed

½ teaspoon white pepper

3 cups fresh corn kernels, cut from the cob, or 2 (10-ounce) packages
    frozen corn kernels

2 cups light cream, scalded

Worcestershire sauce, optional

Salt to taste

Finely chopped parsley, for garnish

HEAT THE BUTTER IN A LARGE SAUCEPAN and cook the onion until translucent. Stir in the flour, and cook over gentle heat for a few minutes. Gradually add the water, stirring, until the mixture is thickened and smooth. Stir in the bouillon and pepper. Add the corn kernels and simmer, covered, for 15 minutes. (If desired, blend in a food processor 2 cupfuls at a time, until it is smooth.)

Stir in the cream. Bring to serving temperature. Season to taste with the Worcestershire sauce and salt. Serve garnished with parsley.

SERVES: 4 TO 6

MAYOR ED KOCH had a slight stroke while he was mayor of New York City, and, while lying bedridden at Gracie Mansion, he heard that he had a visitor. He was soon shocked to learn that Mother Teresa had come to call. He leaped up and put on a bathrobe, saying, "Mother, what are you doing here?" Mother Teresa answered, "You need your friends when you are sick." In honor of friendship, healing, Mother Teresa, and Ed Koch, here is a true comfort soup that bridges all lands and creeds.

Zuppa Maritata

¼ cup minced green onions, with tops

½ cup minced mushrooms

1 tablespoon olive oil

Dash of cayenne pepper

¼ teaspoon salt

¼ teaspoon crumbled dried oregano

1 teaspoon fresh lemon juice

6 cups brown chicken stock, made with extra oregano and garlic

¼ pound vermicelli, broken

1 recipe Chicken Balls, cooked (recipe follows), or 1½ cups diced
    cooked chicken

3 eggs, beaten

1 cup half-and-half

6 tablespoons freshly grated Romano cheese

Salt, black pepper, and minced fresh oregano to taste

Dash of paprika

Minced fresh Italian parsley

Freshly grated Romano cheese

SAUTÉ THE GREEN ONIONS and mushrooms in the oil until soft, sprinkle with the cayenne pepper, salt, oregano, and lemon juice while cooking. Add the stock, bring to a boil, and stir in the vermicelli.

Cook for 7 minutes after the soup comes back to a boil. Reheat with Chicken Balls or diced chicken.

Beat together the eggs and cream, whisk in ½ cup of hot soup and return to rest of soup. Heat, but do not boil.

Add the Romano cheese and adjust seasonings to taste with salt, pepper, and oregano.

Sprinkle with paprika and Italian parsley and pass extra Romano cheese.   SERVES: 6 TO 8

Chicken Balls

1 ½ cups ground white-meat chicken
2 tablespoons finely minced fresh parsley
1 egg, beaten
½ cup fine bread crumbs
1 tablespoon freshly grated Romano cheese
¼ teaspoon each salt and black pepper

MIX TOGETHER ALL INGREDIENTS, form into balls the size of large marbles, and refrigerate several hours. Cook in simmering salted water or broth to cover for 10 minutes.

MAKES APPROXIMATELY: 40

WHILE I WAS ON THE BOOK TOUR for *The Secrets of Jesuit Breadmaking*, I was involved in many early-morning television shows, and after a while they all began to look the same. They usually featured a very bright, attractive anchorwoman, who had read all the material; a very athletic-looking guy who knew a lot about football as her cohost; and an overweight weatherman who served as the butt of many people's jokes, and who joked an awful lot about traffic himself.

Well, I have discovered that the key to these shows is to avoid the guy who specializes in football, because he's usually not very astute. On one talk show, I was asked to arrive at 5:30 in the morning so that I could bake a loaf of bread between 6:00 and 8:00. At 6:00, the anchorwoman came over and introduced me, held up my book, and informed the audience that I would be at a book signing later in the day. She asked me to talk about the history of the Jesuit brothers, and the origins of the book, and then to demonstrate the process of baking—which I did.

After the bread was in the oven, there was really not much left to do, although the cameraperson kept saying to me, "All right! In five seconds, we're going to have a teaser, so, Brother, please do something!" Well, one time I peeked into the oven. Another time I pretended to clean up the sink, and another time I feigned putting my utensils away.

The bread came out about 7:30, and around a quarter of eight, the football cohost with the great jaw came over and ripped into the loaf of bread, started eating, and between bites began the following exchange:

"Brother Curry, let me get this straight. Now, you're a Jesuit. Is that right?"

"Yes, Hank, I am."

"But you're also a Jesuit brother. Is that correct?"

"Yes, that's *also* correct."

"Well, now . . . were your parents Jesuits?"

Needless to say, this stopped me dead in my tracks. And I said, stumbling, "Well . . . no . . . they had a different . . . calling, but . . . it's all in the book." Ever anxious to sell the book, I repeated, "B-b-but it's all in the book."

Producers on the show told me afterward that their telephone lines all lit up like Christmas trees. People were horrified that this guy couldn't figure out that parents of Jesuits couldn't be Jesuits themselves.

While his questions gave me pause, it wasn't the most common misconception I've encountered concerning the Jesuits. Very few people, even within the Catholic world, know that Jesuits have brothers as well as priests. And, indeed, the Jesuits have had brothers for the last 450 years. Once Ignatius of Loyola founded the Society of Jesus, he began to realize the wisdom of having some members whom he would accept into the Society as brothers. By having a group of nonordained members of the institute, they too, in their own nonsacerdotal brotherhood, could spread the word of God through their activities of manual labor, administration, and teaching.

Here's a recipe for Hungarian Goulash that football-loving sidekicks everywhere will enjoy. It was given to me by Janice Majsa, the treasurer of the Jesuit Community at Fairfield University, and a very good friend of mine.

Hungarian Goulash

1 pound beef flank
1 large onion, chopped
2 tablespoons lard
¼ tablespoon paprika
1 tablespoon salt
1 fresh tomato, peeled, seeded, and chopped
2 parsley roots and greens, peeled and chopped
1 green pepper, seeded and diced
2 stalks celery, diced
2 large carrots, diced
2 medium potatoes, peeled and diced

CUT THE MEAT INTO SQUARES. Sauté the onion in the lard, add the paprika, stir well, and then add the meat, salt, tomato, and ¼ cup of water.

Cook slowly for 1 hour, and then add the parsley root, green pepper, celery, and carrots.

Add another cup of water and cook slowly for ½ hour. Add the potatoes, and continue cooking for 15 minutes. Add 1 quart of cold water, let the mixture come to a boil, and cook for another 10 minutes.

SERVES: 6 TO 8

IN THE EARLY 1970S, I was lucky enough to teach at the Dominican Academy in Manhattan. It was there that I was first introduced to the Dominican Sisters of St. Mary of the Springs, Columbus, Ohio, and became friends with Sister Helen Kieren, O.P. Following her travels around the world can be an exhausting task, and since I have known her, she has gone from Rome to Korea, back to New York, and most recently to Chimbote, Peru, where she teaches theater and communications to children. Sister Helen alerts me to the fact that Peru is the second-poorest country in the Western Hemisphere, but that does not stop the sisters from serving a remarkable Peruvian Creole Soup.

Peruvian Creole Soup

1 loin pork chop, about ¾ inch thick (about ½ pound)

1 to 2 teaspoons olive oil

1 medium onion, finely chopped

1 medium tomato, peeled, seeded, and chopped

1 small dried hot red chile, finely crushed

1 small clove garlic, minced or pressed

1 pinch salt

1 pinch ground cumin

½ teaspoon turmeric

2 (14½-ounce) cans chicken broth

2 egg yolks

1 cup half-and-half

Chopped parsley, for garnish

TRIM THE FAT FROM THE PORK CHOP. Cut this fat into small pieces, and reserve it. Cut the meat from the bone and discard the bone. Cut the meat into thin, bite-sized strips.

In a 3-quart saucepan over medium heat, cook the pork fat until it coats the pan; add a little olive oil if needed. Discard any solid pieces of fat. Add the pork strips and onion and cook, stirring, until lightly browned. Mix in the tomato, chile, garlic, salt, cumin, and turmeric.

Add the broth, bring to a boil, cover, reduce heat, and simmer until the pork is very tender, about 30 minutes. Meanwhile, in a small bowl, beat the egg yolks with the half-and-half.

After 30 minutes, gradually whisk about 1 cup of the hot broth into the egg mixture; stir it vigorously into the soup, and continue stirring over medium-low heat until the soup is steaming hot and slightly thickened. Do not boil. Taste, and add salt if needed. Serve sprinkled with parsley.

SERVES: 6 TO 8

IN THE FALL OF 1985, after I had finished filming *The Life of Little Margaret*, I took the train from Città di Costello to Rome, where I attended the beatification of Brother Francis Garate (1857–1929). Brother Garate's life was remarkably similar to that of St. Alphonsus Rodriguez. He was born in Ignatius's hometown of Azpeitia, and two of his blood brothers also became brothers in the Society of Jesus. Brother Garate prayed while he worked, and worked while he prayed. He spent most of his life in Duesto, in Balboa, as a doorkeep.

After the beatification, I walked to the Jesuit headquarters, and stepped onto the roof overlooking St. Peter's. I was above a courtyard and garden, where many Spanish Jesuits had gathered. I soon saw an astonishing sight, as Brother Banderas, an infirmarion, wheeled Father Pedro Arrupe into the courtyard, and the Spanish Jesuits ran from all directions to surround him. In May 1965, Father Arrupe had been elected superior general of the Society of Jesus, the twenty-seventh successor to St. Ignatius, and he held that position until his resignation in September 1983. On that evening, in 1985, we all gathered in a massive refectory, where we began a feast with Garlic Soup.

Garlic Soup

½ cup olive oil

1 large bulb garlic (about 20 cloves), cloves peeled and sliced lengthwise

3 or 4 slices of stale white bread

1 cup water

4 cups homemade beef stock or 3 (10½-ounce) cans beef broth

6 egg yolks, beaten

Salt to taste

White pepper to taste

HEAT THE OIL in a skillet and cook the garlic until it is golden. Remove with a slotted spoon and reserve.

Remove the skillet from the heat and dip each slice of bread in the hot oil, turning it once. Return the skillet to the heat, and sauté each slice until it is golden and crisp. Reserve.

Combine the garlic, water, and stock in a saucepan, and bring to a boil. Reduce the heat and simmer for 45 minutes. Strain and reserve the broth.

Puree the garlic and some of the broth in a food processor. Return the puree to the broth.

Add the egg yolks to 2 cupfuls of the broth, and stir vigorously. Away from the heat, beat the egg mixture into the remaining broth. Season to taste with salt and pepper.

Reheat but do not boil. When serving, ladle the soup over a piece of the reserved bread.

SERVES: 6

Religious life does not exempt you from worldly or human needs. You need haircuts. So some of our men had to be trained as barbers. There's that early awkward period when you're learning how to cut hair; then you finally achieve a certain skill. But for practice along the way, you need victims. So the administrators at Wernersville found a very wise way to handle this problem—employ two kinds of barbers: those in training, and those who had become somewhat accomplished. When you put your slip in for permission to get a haircut, there were two places on it that you could check: one said *"hospites,"* and the other said "non-*hospites.*" *Hospites* meant visitors, so if you were having visitors, you could get a very good barber. If you were not having visitors, then you got a barber-in-training. And they used to tell us, "Look, the difference between a good haircut and a bad haircut is a hat and two weeks." Here's a recipe to console even the most patchily tonsured brother.

Borscht

4 pounds beef chuck
1 pound pork shoulder
2 pounds beef soup bones
Salt and pepper to taste
8 peppercorns
1 bay leaf
6 uncooked beets, stems removed
1 small cabbage, shredded
1 tablespoon fresh lemon juice
½ cup minced dill
½ cup sour cream

WITH A SHARP KNIFE, trim the fat off the beef and pork. Place the meat in a kettle with the bones, cover with water, and add the salt, pepper, peppercorns, and bay leaf. Bring to a boil and reduce the heat; cover and cook for 2 hours. Skim the top with a slotted spoon. Check the meat with a fork to see that it is tender and, if so, remove the meat, cut it into bite-size chunks, and set aside.

In a separate pot, cook the beets in enough water to cover for about 30 minutes. Remove the beets and cut into strips. Put the strips into the meat broth, add the cabbage, return soup to a boil, and simmer for 10 minutes. Add the lemon juice, the chunks of meat, and simmer for another 15 minutes. Add 1 tablespoon of dill and stir. Mix the remaining dill with the sour cream. Place 1 tablespoon of this mixture in each soup bowl, pour borscht over it, and serve.

SERVES: 6 TO 8

HOMELESSNESS IN NEW YORK is a great agony to people of goodwill. The problem is so overwhelming that there seems to be little we can do. On our doorstep on West Fifty-sixth Street in Manhattan there was a woman who, for years, would settle down there late in the evening to seek protection from the elements. We would often ask if she wanted some food or money, but she always refused.

She said very little; she said practically nothing at all. One time, Father Thurston Davis let her know that the new hotel across the street had a public access where she could sit in the warmth. She looked right at him and said—rather articulately—"I don't think they would be *amenable* to that." Those were the only words we ever heard her speak.

My sister Denise came to visit one weekend, and upon our return from being out all day, there was the woman we nicknamed "Annie" sitting in the doorway. I said to Denise, "Now, Denise, don't be frightened of her. We'll go in the side door as we usually do. She has been here for years, and all that time she's not spoken one single word."

Well, when we passed her by, she looked at Denise and said, "Get away from that one-armed man! Get away from him! He's a spy! They're *all* spies in there! They're *all* spies!"

I almost lost Denise to coronary arrest as I hurried her into the building. I was absolutely stunned. I had to ask the rest of the Jesuits to convince Denise that this was not a normal occurrence. Perhaps if Annie had shared this Cream of Fresh Tomato Soup with us, she might have been less suspicious.

Cream of Fresh Tomato Soup

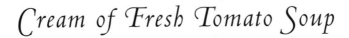

4 large tomatoes, peeled, seeded, and chopped

2 large onions, chopped

2 large carrots, sliced

2 tablespoons sugar

½ bay leaf

¾ teaspoon salt

⅛ teaspoon white pepper

1 (3-inch) strip lemon rind

4 cups canned chicken broth

2 tablespoons butter or margarine, softened

2 tablespoons flour

1⅓ cups half-and-half

Salt to taste

Thinly shredded rind of 2 oranges, for garnish

IN A 4- TO 5-QUART KETTLE, combine the tomatoes, onions, carrots, sugar, bay leaf, salt, pepper, lemon rind, and chicken broth. Bring to a boil over moderately high heat, cover, reduce the heat, and simmer for 30 minutes. Remove and discard the bay leaf and lemon rind.

In a small bowl, mix the butter and flour until smooth; set aside.

Transfer the tomato mixture, a quarter to a third at a time, to a food processor or blender and process until smooth. Return to the kettle over medium heat. Stir in the butter mixture, about a quarter at a time, mixing until the soup thickens and boils.

Remove the soup from heat; add the half-and-half and stir to blend. Return the soup to the heat and cook, stirring occasionally, until steaming hot. Do not boil. Taste and add salt if needed.

To serve cold, remove from heat after thickening, blend in half-and-half, and refrigerate until chilled. Serve sprinkled with orange rind.

SERVES: 4

IN 1977, I WAS LUCKY enough to find an empty loft with a working elevator in the TriBeCa section of Manhattan, and here we began the National Theatre Workshop of the Handicapped. To make all of this happen, I moved into the loft both to live and to start the actors' studio. After successfully qualifying for an artist-in-residence status, I signed the industrial lease. The AIR status allowed me to live in this work space, but the industrial lease offered only five days of heat. Imagine how nippy it was on Saturday morning, not to mention Sunday morning, upon awakening in that loft. Gradually, I was able to build partitions and get space heaters to make the place bearable.

But basically what I had rented was just one large area of undefined space. There was a riser for a toilet, but you had to bring in your own bathroom and your own kitchen. I was blessed with a company of Jesuits who would come down nightly to sand the floors and try to get the place in decent shape so I could move in and begin the National Theatre Workshop of the Handicapped. I also went around and introduced myself to my neighbors. My upstairs neighbor was a remarkable young Jewish woman, a jewelry maker as well as a psychiatric social worker, whose name was Shelly Sheffler. Shelly greeted me warmly in her New York way, and thought it was her job to come down each evening with a big cup of cappucino, which would, of course, keep me up all night. Shelly is one of those people who are interested in everything, but particularly in everything she doesn't know about. That includes Catholicism. I would explain to her what a Jesuit was, and what a Jesuit brother was, what kind of life we led, and what I was trying to do with the National Theatre Workshop of the Handicapped.

One night, my superior, Reverend Leo Daly, S.J., came down from Xavier High School on West Sixteenth Street to have dinner with me. I cooked him dinner and afterward we decided to go out and look at the sights of SoHo, an interesting artists' neighborhood in Manhattan. We stopped in a little local coffeehouse and while we were sitting there we heard a knock on the window. There stood Shelly Sheffler with a friend, apparently our other neighbor. I motioned for her to come in, and said to Leo, "This is my upstairs neighbor, Shelly." She sat down and eventually, in the course of the conversation, Shelly looked at me, looked at Leo, looked back at me, and said, "So, what is your relationship with Leo?" I stared straight into her eyes, tried to get her attention, and replied, "Shelly, Leo is my superior." She gave me a funny look and said, "Rick, I'm so tired of your bad-mouthing yourself. You're as good as anyone else."

It was this incident that motivated me to invite Shelly for dinner, and I served this Red Bell Pepper Soup. Thereafter, Shelly thought that Jesuits had Red Bell Pepper Soup prior to every meal.

Red Bell Pepper Soup *ltc*

yum Oct 2003

3 tablespoons butter or margarine
3 large red bell peppers, seeded and chopped
1 medium onion, finely chopped
¼ teaspoon ground cumin
Pinch of cayenne pepper
2 (14½-ounce) cans chicken broth
2 teaspoons lemon juice
Salt to taste
Italian flat-leaf parsley sprigs, for garnish

IN A 3-QUART saucepan over medium heat, melt the butter. Add the bell peppers and onion and cook, stirring occasionally, until the onion is soft but not browned. Mix in the cumin and cayenne pepper, then add the chicken broth.

Bring to a boil, cover, reduce the heat, and simmer for 20 minutes.

With a slotted spoon, scoop out the vegetables and transfer to a blender or food processor. Add a little of the broth and process until smooth. Return red bell pepper puree to the broth in the cooking pan. Mix in the lemon juice. Taste, and add salt if needed.

Reheat to serving temperature. Serve hot, garnishing each serving with a few leaves of parsley.

SERVES: 4

My mother had a sister who was a Sister of Notre Dame de Namur. Her name in religion was Sister Bernard, but we knew her affectionately as Aunt Katie. Aunt Katie was really a significant force in our family, although we visited her rarely. She exerted her influence through her letter writing, sending elegant, insightful letters to my mother on a regular basis. One of the most touching letters I received years after it had been written. When my mother was leaving our family home for an apartment after my father had retired, she came across the letter that Aunt Katie had written to her on the occasion of my birth. My mother presented this to me when I was thirty years of age. When I looked back and saw the exaltation, and yet the heartache at their little boy being born with one arm, and what it meant to my aunt, I was astounded by the courage and the faith that she had in God that all would be well. When my mother handed me this letter, she told me that Aunt Katie was a prophet, and that all had turned out very well, thank God.

Aunt Katie, or Sister Bernard, was a real institution in the Sisters of Notre Dame, and for many decades taught the eighth-grade boys at St. Aloysius Gonzaga Grammar School in Washington, D.C. The grammar school was next to Gonzaga High School, which is a famous Jesuit prep school in Washington, so not only did she know all the goings-on in the grammar school but she knew all the goings-on in the high school as well. She was devoted to the Jesuits.

Her retirement from teaching was not her own decision, although she had been teaching for almost fifty years at that point, but because the grammar school of St. Aloysius Gonzaga had been closed. Upon the school's closing, a syndicated column was written about my aunt by Robert Considine, who had been one of her students. He said that years later he returned to her classroom and instead of being surprised, she didn't seem to bat an eyelid. She said, "Good morning, Robert, would you like to come in and see the seat where you learned to write so well?" She continued, "I read an article about you recently that said you learned to write at Columbia University. Young man, you learned to write at that very desk." They reflected on his tenure at the school, with Sister Bernard saying, "You won some essay contest because I had So-and-so use his wonderful penmanship so that not only would your content be terrific but the penmanship would be beautiful, too." He asked her, "Sister Bernard, whatever happened to that So-and-so that did such beautiful penmanship?" "Oh," she replied, "he's in prison now for forgery."

You would think that a sister in the old tradition would have some effect on her students, but I really was not prepared for her wake and funeral. So many generations of men came up to tell me what a great influence she was while they were under her care. Even years later, when they came back from World War II or from Korea, they would go to visit her for counsel, and she was always there for them.

When she left St. Aloysius, Sister Bernard was stationed at St. Camilla's in nearby Silver Spring, Maryland, and later she was joined in that convent by my own sister. It was there that my Aunt Katie died in the company of my sister.

She was buried from the upper Church of St. Aloysius (an uncommon event in those days), with a sanctuary filled with many priests, and two bishops, who were all former students. After the funeral mass, the Gonzaga Jesuit Community offered us lunch that began with this delicious vegetable soup. Aunt Katie would have approved.

Swiss Lentil, Ham, and Vegetable Soup

¼ cup dried mushrooms

2 leeks

2 tablespoons butter or margarine

2 medium carrots, chopped

2 medium onions, slivered

1 stalk celery, thinly sliced

1 clove garlic, minced or pressed

10 cups water

2½ cups dried lentils, rinsed and drained (about 1 pound)

1 medium potato, finely diced

1 large tomato, peeled and chopped

4 smoked ham hocks (2½ to 3 pounds)

¾ cup chopped parsley

¼ teaspoon white pepper

1 teaspoon crushed mustard seed

1 bay leaf

Salt to taste

2 hard-cooked eggs, shredded

PLACE THE MUSHROOMS IN A SMALL BOWL and cover with hot water; let stand until soft (30 minutes to 1 hour).

Meanwhile, cut off the root ends of the leeks; remove and discard coarse outer leaves. Cut off and discard the green tops so that leeks are about 9 inches long. Split lengthwise from the leafy end, cutting to within 1 inch of root end. Soak in cold water for several minutes; then separate the leaves under cold running water to rinse away any clinging grit; drain. Slice about ¼ inch thick.

In a 6- to 8-quart kettle over medium heat, melt the butter.

Add the leeks, carrots, onions, celery, and garlic and cook, stirring often, until they are soft but not browned.

To the vegetables add the water, lentils, potato, tomato, ham hocks, ½ cup of the parsley, the pepper, mustard seed, and bay leaf. Bring to a boil. Meanwhile, drain the mushrooms and chop coarsely; add to the lentil mixture. When it begins to boil, cover, reduce heat, and simmer until ham is very tender (3 to 3½ hours).

Remove and discard the bay leaf. Remove the ham hocks. Puree about 2 cups of the lentils and vegetables in a blender or food processor; then return to the soup. When the ham hocks are cool enough to handle, discard bones and skin; return the ham in large chunks to the soup. Taste, and add salt if needed. Reheat if necessary.

Serve hot, garnishing each serving wth hard-cooked egg and some of the remaining chopped parsley.

SERVES: 6 TO 8

YOUNG DOMINIC COLLINS left County Cork for the Continent in 1586, because there were no careers for young Catholics in Ireland. He enlisted in the army of Philip Emmanuel de Vaudemont, Duke of Mer-Coeur, a member of the Catholic League who was fighting against the Huguenots in Brittany. Later, he found himself in the service of Spain, and there met a Jesuit from his homeland. Collins announced his desire to do more with his life, as he was disaffected by the military. He entered the Society as a brother and made his first vows in 1601, in Santiago de Compostela. Seven months later he was assigned to accompany a priest back to Ireland, where the Catholic Church was outlawed by the British. Shortly thereafter, he was captured, thrown into prison, and sent back to Cork, where he was hanged. Eyewitnesses said that he wore the Jesuit cassock, and cheerfully climbed the platform, where he said that he had returned home to preach his Catholic faith. He dangled for over three hours before the rope snapped and dropped his body to the ground. He was stripped and left naked until the night, when Catholics gathered up his body to bury him. We celebrate his memory with Irish Potato and Broccoli Soup.

Irish Potato and Broccoli Soup

2 tablespoons butter

2 onions, finely chopped

2 potatoes, peeled and cubed

1 head broccoli, washed and cut into 1-inch pieces

1 tablespoon dried tarragon

Salt and pepper to taste

2 quarts chicken stock or water

1 cup finely chopped fresh parsley

MELT THE BUTTER in a kettle and sauté the onions until translucent. Add the potatoes, broccoli, tarragon, salt, pepper, and stock. Bring to a boil, reduce the heat, cover, and cook for 20 minutes over medium heat. Add the parsley.

SERVES: 6 TO 8

Christmas

Dearest Lord, teach me to be generous.

Teach me to serve you as you deserve; to give

and not to count the cost; to toil and not to

seek for rest; to labor and not to ask reward,

save to know that I am doing your will, oh God.

Amen.

ST. IGNATIUS LOYOLA

ONE OF THE PERKS of living in a Jesuit community is that you have access to great stories. At times it is impossible to track down the origins of Jesuit lore because, like all stories, these can take on a life of their own—in content and style, they often alter the cold hard facts of history. But I know of one story that doesn't suffer from this inaccuracy because I was able to follow the trail to its original source.

One Sunday morning at our community liturgy the Reverend John W. Donohue, S.J., mentioned the sufferings of John Havas (1908–1994) in his homily. Havas, a Hungarian Jesuit missioner to China, was arrested by Communists and imprisoned there for twenty-two months, from September 1952 until he was expelled in May 1954. I didn't get all this information from the homily—I did a little research of my own. Father Donohue had referred to a Christmas letter written by Father Havas years after his imprisonment, and it fascinated me enough to make me want to read it myself. I asked James Martin, a young Jesuit priest, if he had ever heard of John Havas before that morning's homily. He recalled that there was an account of Havas's life in George Anderson's wonderful book on Jesuits in prison. (Both James and George are associate editors of *America* magazine, a weekly journal of opinion sponsored by the U.S. Jesuits.) Off I scurried to look at George's book, where I found the description of John Havas's "Christmas Eve in a Shanghai Prison" that had been part of a 1991 Christmas letter he had sent to his friends. A copy of it had been given to James Dolan, a Jesuit who had worked with Father Havas

from 1972 to 1978 at Loyola House of retreats in Morristown, New Jersey. So the trail started at morning worship, went through four Jesuits, and ended in my reading of this profoundly moving Christmas story.

In 1952, John Havas deeply desired to offer Mass on Christmas Eve. He was told by the Chinese prison authorities that they would consider his request if he would sign a confession and give up the names of his former students. Without hesitation he responded, "No thank you. Forget it!" This infuriated his captors and they retaliated by brutally dragging him out of his cell in the middle of night and throwing him into a pit filled with the smell of cadavers and human excrement. He cried out in despair, "My God, my God, why have you forsaken me?" In his darkness, a great grace enveloped him and the word *Bethlehem* entered his consciousness, and he realized what a fool he had been for doubting the goodness of God. In his wretched state, he identified with the poverty of the Son of God being born in a stable. In that moment an enormous feeling of gratitude flooded his heart as he realized that he had not been left alone. He felt the presence of God so vividly that he thought his heart would break because of his unbounded joy. At the end of his long life, John Havas claimed that the Christmas Eve of 1952 in a Chinese prison was the happiest day he had known.

Christmas has that power, and meditating on Bethlehem can bring that rapture.

IN 1985, I was invited by Queen Sofia of Spain, the honorary president of the Royal Board on Education and Care of Handicapped Persons, to participate in a conference on disability and the arts. The organizers of the conference asked me to arrive three days early, which I did. They had arranged for me to stay in a bed-and-breakfast in downtown Madrid. After a tiring early-morning flight, I arrived in Madrid at 6:30 in the morning, and despite my limited familiarity with Spanish, I quickly found my *pensión*. I announced myself to the staff there, and while lost in thoughts of a warm shower and the comfort of my room, I was informed that I had lost my reservation. The convention staff had booked the reservation based upon the date of my flight, without allowing for the fact that I would be arriving a day later in Spain. There was no room for me.

By now it was midmorning, and I was in downtown Madrid with very little Spanish at my disposal and no place to stay. I thought that perhaps there might be a Jesuit community in Madrid and that they could house me, so I found a phone book and sought out Jesuits. Unfortunately, the phone book was of no help, so I decided to start out for another *pensión*. After much anxiety and a great deal of walking, I located an available room. Finally, I was able to unpack, shower, and relax in some comfort and security. Now, the difficulty was that the conference staff wouldn't know how to find me, and with the conference on Monday, I would have to spend the weekend on my own in Madrid. Needless to say, it was an adventurous weekend. I ran into some difficulty when it came time for me to eat, and I was a little shy about ordering in Spanish, but I did find a restaurant that had food out on display. I saw a bowl of soup—rich potato and kale soup—which I pointed to, and the waitress, correctly interpreting my gesture, gave me a bowl of the soup and some wonderful, crusty bread. I've never had potato and kale soup since without thinking of the comfort and reassurance it gave me back then. When I returned to New York, I told a fellow Jesuit about my escapades in Madrid, and he informed me that there were at least twenty-five Jesuit houses in Madrid, three of which were guesthouses for visiting Jesuits. In my distress, I had forgotten that a Spaniard founded the Society of Jesus.

If my taste buds have a good memory, this recipe duplicates my Madrid experience.

Potato and Kale Soup

5 tablespoons olive oil
4 medium potatoes, peeled and sliced
8 cups water
¼ pound chorizo or other garlic-flavored smoked sausage
1 pound fresh kale, woody stems removed, rinsed, dried, and chopped
Salt and pepper to taste

HEAT THE OLIVE OIL in a soup kettle and stir in the potatoes until they are well coated. Add the water, bring to a boil, and cook for 25 minutes, until the potatoes are very tender.

Prick the sausage in several places with a fork, and while the potatoes are cooking, simmer it in a little water over low heat for 15 minutes. Drain it on absorbent paper, and then slice into ½-inch rounds.

Puree the potatoes in a food processor, then return to the kettle. Add the reserved sausage and stir in the kale. Bring to a boil, reduce the heat, and simmer, covered, for 5 minutes, until the kale is tender. Season to taste with salt and pepper.

SERVES: 6 TO 8

My experience with the elderly, particularly in the Society of Jesus, is that happy old Jesuits were happy as young Jesuits. There are very few surprises. Those Jesuits who had a zest for life while young seem to have a zest for life now. What I pray for is that I will have intellectual curiosity and enthusiasm now, so that I might continue to have it when I'm old.

When I was stationed at St. Joseph's University, Father Tom Stokes celebrated his Golden Jubilee in the Society of Jesus. Father Stokes had been an elocution and English teacher for years at St. Joseph's, and his own delivery had style—he was quite a raconteur. We had a lovely Jubilee feast, to which only Jesuits were invited, and at the end of the meal, he stood up and thanked us all for coming and communally celebrating his fifty years of service to the Society of Jesus. It made him think, he said, of another fiftieth anniversary. "Today, I am reminded of my own parents. When they celebrated their fiftieth anniversary of marriage, my father sent my mother sixteen red roses. My mother was baffled. She said, 'I could understand a dozen roses, I could even understand fifty roses, but why sixteen?'" And Father Stokes said that his father looked into his mother's eyes lovingly and said, "'Because sixteen was the age you were when I first met you, and I can no longer afford what you are today.'" Then Father Stokes concluded, "And today is not the first day in my life that I am grateful those two met."

The following mellow soup will keep you happy over the years—good eating before the fire on any winter night of your life.

Cheddar Cheese Soup

4 tablespoons butter

1 tablespoon olive oil

4 carrots, peeled and diced

2 green bell peppers, seeded and diced

3 tablespoons flour

½ cup powdered milk

3 cups vegetable stock

½ cup sherry

2 cups grated Cheddar cheese

1 ½ cups milk

½ tablespoon paprika

½ cup finely chopped parsley

Salt and pepper to taste

HEAT THE BUTTER AND OIL in a kettle and sauté the carrots and green bell peppers for 5 minutes. Sprinkle the flour and powdered milk over, and gradually add the stock. Make sure that the consistency is smooth, at which time add the sherry, cheese, milk, paprika, parsley, salt, and pepper. Cook, stirring, for 3 minutes.

SERVES: 6

WERNERSVILLE IS SITUATED in the Pennsylvania Dutch section of Pennsylvania, and the Jesuit novitiate there bordered the property of St. John's Hain's Lutheran Church. As a matter of fact, their cemetery was on the other side of our fence, beyond the Juniors' Arbor. (Juniors were the young Jesuits engaged in their collegiate studies.) On a brisk fall day, I loved nothing more than to walk through this ancient cemetery, reading the names on the gravestones. Most provocative were: EMMA—DEAD AT 3 and WILLIAM, HER BROTHER—DEAD AT 1. Influenza had torn through these small German communities and this cemetery recorded their loss. The church, painted in a beautifully understated black-and-white interior motif, remained open at all times, and often served as a retreat for novices caught out in the rain while coming home from a winter's walk.

This was the early 1960s, and the ecumenical council had yet to convene, so there was not much sharing between our communities. On the contrary, stories of prejudice abounded, and the Pennsylvania Dutch probably looked at us with great puzzlement. In 1963, Wernersville celebrated its one hundredth anniversary as a borough, and St. John's Hain's Lutheran wanted to observe the occasion with music. They wanted to sing Handel's "Hallelujah Chorus," and while they had a wonderful choir, they would need more male voices for this difficult piece. They sent us an invitation, asking if we would join them for this performance, and we, wanting to be good neighbors, assented.

Two rehearsals were arranged prior to the performance, and the conductor was to be one of our junior scholastics. Wednesday evening, we arrived for our first rehearsal promptly at seven, wearing our long black habits. Both Lutherans and Catholics were understandably nervous, but they greeted us warmly, and we got down to business. In music, we discovered that we had more in common than not. Afterward, the wonderful women of the St. John's Hain's choir—superb bakers all—brought out their blue-ribbon pies and cakes for our refreshment, in order to show their gratitude. To their amazement, the young men of our novice and junior choir did not gorge themselves on their desserts—this due to our rule against eating outside of prescribed mealtimes. Eventually, one of our juniors realized that charity took precedence over the letter of this edict; and so the word quickly spread among us that we could, in fact, dig in, which we did with gusto.

The next Friday, the more fervent among us got permission ahead of time to enjoy these refreshments. Our second rehearsal was even more of a success than our first, but to our great disappointment, there were no cakes or pies awaiting us. Those treats were saved for the celebration itself, at which the combined choirs of St. John's Hain's and St. Isaac Jogues Novitiate welcomed Wernersville Borough's second century before hundreds of local citizens. Afterward, a potluck dinner was held, at which I first enjoyed this Dried Corn Chowder.

Dried Corn Chowder

1½ cups dried corn, rinsed

4 cups homemade chicken stock or 3 (10½-ounce) cans
    chicken broth

6 slices bacon, diced

3 medium onions, chopped

4 cups milk

2 teaspoons sugar

Salt and pepper to taste

COMBINE THE DRIED CORN and stock in a large saucepan. Bring to a boil, remove from heat, and allow it to stand, covered, for 2 hours. Return the liquid to a boil, reduce the heat, and simmer the corn, covered, for 45 minutes, until it is tender.

Render the bacon in a skillet, then drain it on absorbent paper and reserve. Cook the onion in the bacon fat until it is translucent. Add the onion, drippings, milk, and sugar to the saucepan. Heat the chowder thoroughly. Season to taste with salt and pepper. Serve garnished with the reserved bacon.

SERVES: 6 TO 8

I HAVE ALWAYS BEEN DELIGHTED by other people's sense of humor. I have a dear friend named John Hawley, an English professor at Santa Clara University. I got to know him while we were both in New York completing our doctoral dissertations. When I was visiting John at Santa Clara, he introduced me to some friends, and he asked them if they had ever read my book, *The Secrets of Jesuit Breadmaking.* He told them, "*The Secrets of Jesuit Breadmaking* is a recipe book to which eighty Jesuit brothers have contributed their recipes, but the recipes themselves have come directly from the Blessed Mother. She dictated each of the recipes to these brothers." Whatever its source, divine or otherwise, the following two soup recipes are perfect for the deepening nights of December.

Clam and Mushroom Soup

2 medium leeks, thinly sliced (with the white and some green)

1 large clove garlic, minced

2 teaspoons minced fresh tarragon

2 tablespoons butter and/or rendered chicken fat

1 tablespoon unbleached flour

2 (7½-ounce) cans minced clams

½ cup dry vermouth

⅓ cup mushroom concentrate

¾ pound mushrooms, sliced

Salt to taste

White pepper to taste

⅓ cup sour cream, or to taste

Minced fresh parsley and/or chives, for garnish

Sour cream, for garnish

Garlic or cheese croutons, for garnish

COOK THE LEEKS, garlic, and tarragon in the butter or chicken fat in a covered pot until the leeks are soft. Sprinkle with flour and continue to cook, while stirring, for 3 minutes.

Drain the clam liquor and add water, to make 2 cups. Gradually stir the liquid into the leek mixture, along with the vermouth and mushroom concentrate. Add the mushrooms, salt, and pepper.

Cover the mixture and bring it to a gentle boil; lower the heat and simmer for 10 minutes, or until the mushrooms are tender. Add the sour cream and the reserved clams. Reheat and adjust seasonings to taste. Sprinkle the soup with parsley and garnish with croutons and dollops of sour cream.

SERVES: 4

Oyster Stew

3 dozen medium oysters, finely chopped
4 tablespoons butter
1 onion, minced
1 cup finely chopped celery stalks
1 cup finely chopped parsley
1 tablespoon flour
3 cups milk
1 bay leaf
½ teaspoon ground nutmeg
1 teaspoon ground coriander
1 cup heavy cream
½ cup sherry, optional
Salt and pepper to taste

RESERVE THE LIQUID from the oysters and set aside.

In a saucepan, melt the butter and sauté the onion until golden. Add the celery and parsley, stir in the flour, then gradually pour in the milk. Add the bay leaf, nutmeg, and coriander, as well as the oysters and the reserved liquid.

Bring the mixture to a boil. Reduce to very low heat, and then add the cream and sherry. Season with salt and pepper as desired. Let simmer for 1 minute.

SERVES: 6 TO 8

WHEN I WAS IN THE FIRST GRADE, a woman on our street who was the president of the block Rosary Society, Mrs. Patterson, affectionately known as Monsignor, learned that the right forearm of St. Francis Xavier was coming to the Cathedral of St. Peter and Paul in Philadelphia for veneration. Because I'm missing a right forearm, Mrs. Patterson thought it would be a good idea to tell my mother about this event. My mother thanked her.

Now, my mother had a very healthy theology. She certainly wasn't expecting any miracles, but she was so devoted to St. Francis Xavier and to the Society of Jesus that she thought it would not be a bad idea for me to go and venerate the relic. So she wrote a letter asking for me to be excused from my classes in the first grade.

My first-grade teacher, Sister Philip Neri, I.H.M., had an equally good theology. She also thought that it would be a good thing for me to go and venerate the arm, but she also didn't consider a miracle a plausible outcome, nor did she make any connection between the right forearm that was traveling around the world and my missing right forearm.

My classmates, on the other hand, were receptive for entirely different reasons. They were *praying* for a miracle. And so, when my mother came to pick me up at the classroom door to take me to the cathedral, it was with high expectations that my fellow students watched me leave the room.

When I arrived at the cathedral, I was amazed to see how many people were in that church. There was a serpentine line going up and down the aisles for people who wanted to venerate the relic. There were so many people that an announcement was made that you would no longer be able to kiss the relic, but merely touch it, because of constraints on time.

My mother deposited me in a pew while she stood in line. I quickly fell asleep. Some time later, she awakened me and told me it was time to go, and we walked up the aisle. There were several clergymen hovering around the relic, and when they saw me, they said, "Oh, no, no, he can kiss it."

To my shock, under the glass was not a regular arm, but a skeleton of an arm, and now they wanted me to *kiss* it. Well, I scrunched up my face and pressed my lips against the glass, but at the same time I pressed the stump of my right arm into my ribs in hopes that it would not grow.

Going back to school on the trolley, I kept looking down to see if there was any movement at all in my arm. There wasn't. When I walked into class sans miracle, my classmates let me know their disappointment. They suggested that somehow I wasn't worthy of a miracle.

That same acknowledgment, however, was not shared by my sister. When I got home that night, my sister was hiding behind the drapes in the living room. She peeked out from behind them, and when she saw that no miracle had occurred, she declared, "Oh, great! Because I like you the way you are."

That affirmation is something I really have never forgotten.

Years later, on the Feast of St. Francis Xavier, I invited some Jesuit friends to the theater loft and served them this offbeat but delightful soup. Of course, my guests had to listen to my Francis Xavier story before we supped.

Bongo Bongo Soup

1 bunch of spinach (about 12 ounces)

3 tablespoons butter or margarine

1 small clove garlic, minced or pressed

2 cups milk

1 (10-fluid-ounce) jar fresh oysters

1 cup heavy cream

1 teaspoon Worcestershire sauce

¾ teaspoon salt

⅛ teaspoon white pepper

REMOVE AND DISCARD THE STEMS from well-washed spinach (you should have about 8 cups of leaves). Place the spinach in a large saucepan and stir, uncovered, over medium heat with no added liquid until the spinach is limp (3 to 5 minutes). Drain well, pressing out excess moisture. Chop spinach coarsely and set aside.

In a 2- to 3-quart saucepan over medium heat, melt the butter. Add the garlic and cook, stirring, until golden (do not brown). Add the milk and heat until it steams. Add the oysters (with any liquid) and poach until the edges ruffle (2 to 3 minutes). Remove from the heat.

Transfer the oyster mixture to a blender or food processor. Add the cooked spinach. Process until very smooth.

Return the spinach and oyster mixture to the cooking pan. Add ⅔ cup of the cream and the Worcestershire sauce, salt, and pepper. Stir occasionally over medium heat until blended and steaming hot. Do not boil.

Whip remaining cream until not quite stiff. Put soup in heatproof bowls. Spoon on the whipped cream. Broil about 4 inches from heat until golden brown (2 to 3 minutes). Serve immediately.

SERVES: 6

ONE DAY IN THE NOVITIATE, I was found just wandering aimlessly along a corridor. Brother Reilly stopped me and said, "Brother Curry, where are you going and what are you doing?"

I admitted to Brother Reilly, who was a senior brother and in charge of the treasurer's office, "Brother, I'm really just walking around."

He admonished me, saying, "*Never . . . just . . . walk . . . around . . . Brother!* People may spot you as aimless in life. Always carry a book or a piece of paper as if you're delivering something to someone. Otherwise, they'll grab you to do more work."

You can imagine my delight during the two years in the novitiate watching Brother Reilly walk up and down the corridors, many times carrying a piece of paper, as if he were delivering an urgent message.

Here's a no-nonsense soup that Brother Reilly would indeed walk down the hall to eat.

Green Bean and Ham Soup

1 ham bone, with its meat (about 1 pound)

4 cups water

2 cups cut-up green beans (cut into 1-inch pieces)

1 medium onion, thinly sliced

1 large potato, peeled and diced

¼ cup finely chopped parsley

½ teaspoon dried summer savory

½ teaspoon salt

¼ teaspoon pepper

1 cup light cream

COMBINE THE HAM BONE and water in a soup kettle. Bring to a boil, reduce the heat, and simmer for 1½ hours.

Remove the meat from the bone, chop it, and return it to the broth; discard the bone. Add the remaining ingredients except for the cream.

Return the mixture to a boil, reduce the heat, and simmer for 20 minutes, until the beans are tender. Stir in the cream and bring the soup to serving temperature.

SERVES: 4 TO 6

BROTHER FRANK DIXON, S.J., was a very amiable old man. His bedroom was off the first-floor corridor, and in the summer, the transom would be open over his door. When you passed his room in the summer, it sounded as though a very active beehive were humming along inside. In fact, Brother kept a collection of fans—astonishingly, fifteen to twenty fans. He always said that he was merely collecting and repairing these fans, but the truth was that Brother was a pack rat. The following summer, he had a slight seizure in his room, and the emergency medical service had to be called. To save face (or, rather, to make a bad situation into an edifying one), Brother Reilly ran out to greet the ambulance drivers shouting, "Come quickly, Brother has had a seizure in our storeroom!"

What follows is a simple soup in honor of this much-loved fan collector.

Chicken Leg Noodle Soup

4 chicken legs (with thighs)
10 cups water
1 large celery stalk, with leaves, cut in half
Salt to taste
2 cups thin egg noodles

IN A LARGE SOUP POT, cover the legs with water (allow 2½ cups of water for each chicken leg and 1 leg per person). Add the celery.

Bring the water to a boil. Reduce the heat to a low boil. Cover and simmer 1 hour. Salt the stock to taste.

Remove the legs and celery. Pick the meat from the legs, discarding the skin and bones. Add the chicken meat to the stock. Bring stock to a boil and add the noodles.

Reduce the heat to medium and boil the soup, uncovered, 7 to 10 minutes, or until the noodles are al dente.

SERVES: 4

ON ONE OCCASION, I left Manhattan for New Jersey to give a lecture on responsible sexuality to a group of disabled college students. A member of the panel was a woman named Jamie Sue Casabianca. Jamie Sue had called me earlier, wondering if she could hitch a ride with me, because she had directions to Ramapo College in New Jersey from Manhattan but no means of transportation. I told her that would be perfect.

The next morning, I arrived at Fourteenth Street and Avenue B to wait for Jamie Sue. Of course, I had never met her. There was no one there, although she had promised me that she would not be a minute late. While I was sitting there waiting, I looked into my rearview mirror and saw a woman halfway down the block with a guide dog. I thought, Aha, I bet that's Jamie Sue Casabianca, and I never realized that she was blind.

I put the car in reverse, drove back, and rolled down the window, saying, "Jamie Sue?" She said, "Yes?" And with that she opened the car door, put her guide dog in the back, and sat down in the front seat, as we started toward the George Washington Bridge.

We had been riding for some time when I said to her, "Jamie Sue, I'm a bit taken aback, because I was under the impression that you would be the one piloting me to this college, and I didn't realize that you were blind." "Well," she said, "I have the directions in my head," and, sure enough, she did: we arrived at the college without any difficulty at all. But as we were going across the George Washington Bridge, she said to me, "Rick, I can't discern what your disability is." "Oh, I'm sorry," I said, "I have a missing right forearm." She said, "You do?" I said, "yes," and she said, "And you were worried about my giving directions? I should be terrified that you're at the wheel."

Bread Dumplings

3 cups ½-inch bread cubes, cut from stale bread
½ teaspoon baking powder
¼ cup flour
¾ teaspoon salt
¼ teaspoon pepper
½ cup milk
1 egg
1 tablespoon melted butter or vegetable oil
1 tablespoon finely chopped parsley
Grating or two of onion

IN A MIXING BOWL, combine and blend the bread cubes, baking powder, flour, salt, and pepper. In another mixing bowl, using a rotary beater, combine and blend thoroughly the remaining ingredients. Using a fork, stir the liquid ingredients into the dry ingredients until the mixture has the consistency of a light but lumpy dough.

Onto the surface of the simmering soup, spoon the dough in individual portions. Cook the dumplings, covered, for 8 minutes. Serve them at once.

Matzo Balls

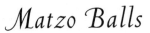

⅓ cup chicken fat
2 eggs
1 cup matzo meal
1 teaspoon salt
⅓ cup water
Boiling salted water or chicken stock

IN A MIXING BOWL, combine the chicken fat, eggs, matzo meal, and salt. Using a fork, blend these ingredients well. Gradually add the ⅓ cup water, beating constantly, until the batter is stiff.

Refrigerate the batter for 2 hours. With your hands moistened in cold water, quickly mold walnut-size balls of the dough.

Drop them into boiling water to cover. Cook, covered, for 30 minutes; drain. Serve the matzo balls in clear soup.

I WAS REFLECTING THE OTHER DAY on a Jesuit teacher of mine at St. Joseph's Prep, Father Frank Dougherty. He was probably one of the best teachers I've ever had. The curriculum at St. Joseph's was in the old style of the *Ratio Studiorum,* the Jesuit plan of studies first published in 1599 that was found in all the Jesuit high schools in the United States at that time. In our freshman year, we had a fixed program. At St. Joseph's Prep, in order to cut down on confusion and wasted time, we students remained in the classroom, while our teachers rotated through the classes. Father Frank Dougherty was a tall man, who I suspect had been quite a good athlete in his day. He was our homeroom teacher, which meant that he taught us catechism, then launched into two periods of Latin and one period of English. On Thursdays, he also had us for a very strange period called health. I suspect it was the Jesuits' nod to the state curricular requirements. In fact, we were allowed to use this period to go over to the Gesu Church, where we could make ourselves available for confession.

Father Dougherty really had an enormous impact on me. In English class, he had us read *The Catcher in the Rye,* by J. D. Salinger. I don't remember much about the novel from that reading when I was a freshman, but I do remember that Father Dougherty said this was the kind of novel you should read again and again in your lifetime. He said that about several novels, but I remember that he mentioned this one in particular. He said that it would give you whole new insights when you were fifty years of age. Well, I'm slightly past fifty, and I had just recalled what he said when I saw the book on the shelf in a store and thought, I should follow Frank Dougherty's suggestion and reread this now that I'm past fifty. It was an astounding revelation. I suspect that as a high school boy, I identified with Holden Caulfield's rebelliousness. But looking at it now, I think Holden Caulfield is a saint. Yes, I know that he moaned and groaned about various things that he found to be phony, but I also think that his charity toward people was astounding. This is what you do when you reflect at fifty. What looks rebellious when you are young looks virtuous when you're old. Wisdom can only come with age and experience, and I think that what we miss most in our society is not listening to those who have had that experience, and who enjoy old age.

The oldest man I knew when I was a little boy was Mr. Baddit, a delightful retired French chef. After coming to Philadelphia from Lyon as a young man, he worked in hotel kitchens for over forty years. I would sit on his porch for hours listening to his stories about food and cooking. He was no longer cooking, but his wife would set up TV tables on the porch and serve a delicious cream of chicken soup. He would always wink at me and then compliment his wife on the tastiness of the soup.

Glorified Cream of Chicken Soup

Bones of 1 or 2 chickens, with giblets (leftover chicken welcome)

1 onion, stuck with 4 cloves

1 celery stalk, diced

2 carrots, peeled and sliced

1 turnip, peeled and sliced

1 leek, washed and diced

1 bay leaf

1 bunch parsley, washed

1 teaspoon dried thyme

1 teaspoon dried tarragon

8 cups water

3 tablespoons butter

4 tablespoons flour

1 large or 2 small truffles, minced, plus juice

½ cup Madeira wine

1 tablespoon anisette

2 egg yolks, mixed with 1 cup heavy cream

PUT THE CHICKEN BONES, giblets, onion, celery, carrots, turnip, leek, bay leaf, parsley, thyme, and tarragon in a kettle. Add the water, cover, and bring to a boil. Reduce the heat and simmer for 1½ hours. Discard the bones and skin, bay leaf, and cloves. Puree the remaining contents of the kettle. Melt the butter in the emptied kettle, and add the flour and some of the liquid. Gradually add the balance of the liquid, stirring. Add the truffle and juice, the wine, and the anisette. Bring to a near boil and add the egg and cream mixture.

SERVES: 6 TO 8

AFTER DINNER AT THE NOVITIATE, those of us who were not assigned to washing dishes or cleaning up the refectory would gather outside the cloister doors. There the maniductor, the novice who was first among equals, would assign us randomly into bands of three, and we would go out together for a recreational walk. One evening, my group included Brother Jimmy Redington. Brother Redington, who is now Father Redington, was a scholastic novice from Scranton with an enormous, inviting sense of humor and an infectious laugh, but also a very generous heart.

   We were walking behind the building where there was an entrance to what we called the Via Pastrina, when we saw the ice truck drive up. The ice truck was a great mystery to us, because even as a brother who worked in the kitchen I really had no idea as to the reason for these ice deliveries. The ice man's name was Amos. He was a Pennsylvania Dutchman who was always accompanied by his rather stocky wife. In a moment of largesse, Brother Redington said, "Amos, would you like us to help you take those blocks of ice off the truck?" Amos, of course, said, "Yes, that would be wonderful." And to be further friendly and chatty with Amos, Brother Redington remarked on his red lumber jacket, saying, "Amos, when I was in the world I had a jacket just like that." Amos looked at his wife, looked at us, shook his head, and said, "Where the hell do you think you are now, Mars?"

We were so drunk with laughter that we nearly dropped those huge blocks of ice as we put them in iceboxes next to our cold cellar. We quickly sobered up when we saw the astonishing number of potatoes that the cold cellar held. No wonder we had so many potato soups. However, this is one of my favorites.

Mushroom-Potato Soup

1 recipe Irish Potato and Broccoli Soup (page 58) (prepare without
  broccoli)
1 cup finely minced mushrooms
¼ cup minced celery
¼ cup minced green onions
3 tablespoons butter
⅓ teaspoon garlic powder
½ teaspoon fresh lemon juice
Dash of ground oregano
1 cup half-and-half
Salt and pepper to taste
Paprika, for garnish
Minced fresh dill or parsley, for garnish

PREPARE THE POTATO SOUP and set aside. Sauté the mushrooms, celery, and green onions in the butter until soft, sprinkling
with garlic powder, lemon juice, and oregano.

Add some of the prepared soup and puree. Combine this with
the remainder of the soup, add half-and-half and heat, but do not
bring to a boil. Add salt and pepper to taste. Sprinkle with paprika
and dill.

SERVES: 4 TO 6

WHEN I WAS IN THE FIRST GRADE at St. Francis De Sales grammar school in Philadelphia, my first-grade teacher, Sister Philip Neri, I.H.M., announced to the class that anyone who wanted to take piano lessons was to bring a note from his or her mother. I went home and informed my mother, "I would like your permission to take piano lessons." My mother said, "Ricky, I don't think that would be a good idea, because I think it really takes two hands to learn to play the piano, and you were born with only one." I said, "Oh, no, that's not what I need. Sister said all I really need is a note from you." My mother surrendered to my will, wrote the letter, and gave me permission to take piano lessons.

The following day, Sister Philip Neri read the names of the students who were to go across the street to meet Sister Mary Innocence, who would begin our instruction in music. My name was not on the list. With a certain amount of six-year-old umbrage, I went up to Sister and said, "Sister, you didn't call my name and my mother gave me permission for piano lessons." Sister looked right at me and said, "Yes, Richard, I know your mother gave you permission for piano lessons, but there were so many students that signed up this year that Sister Mary Innocence can only take girls." That made a lot of sense to me, so that was the end of my quest for piano lessons.

In the fourth grade, our grammar school was the first Catholic school mainstreamed for the blind. Our pastor, Bishop Joseph McShay, opened a small semidetached house across the street called St. Lucy's Blind School. The blind students who attended that school came over to our classes for instruction in history, geography, religion, and spelling, and they would go back to St. Lucy's for Braille, mathematics, and typewriting. But on Friday afternoons, the blind students went down to the auditorium to learn tap dancing. I thought that would be much more exciting than just taking some rudimentary art classes on a Friday afternoon, so I asked Sister if I could join the blind students and take tap dancing. Sister said, "No, I'm sorry, Richard, you can't take tap dancing because you're not blind." Now, I couldn't take piano lessons because I wasn't a girl, and I couldn't take tap dancing lessons because I wasn't blind.

Years later, after I entered the Jesuits, I was stationed back in Philadelphia. While down at John Wanamaker's department store, now defunct, in Philadelphia, I came across two nuns. One of them approached me and said, "Richard, Richard Curry?" I said, "Yes?" and she said, "I'm Sister Philip Neri, your first-grade teacher." I was startled, and stammered out, "My God, Sister, I thought you were dead." She quickly corrected me, saying, "Listen, young man, when I taught you in the first grade, I was nineteen years old." I said, "Sister, I'm astounded you could remember me." "Remember you?" she replied. "Not only do I remember you, but also that your mother gave you permission for piano lessons. We didn't know what to do about it, so my Superior and I stayed up after night prayer to figure it out and finally Mother said to me, 'How many boys have signed up?' and I told her 'Five.' She said, 'Fine. Tell them they can't take it until next year.'"

Years later, I was stationed in New York while earning my doctorate in theater arts at New York University. I went to see the musical *Grease* and was surprised to find in the program the name of one of my grammar school classmates, Steven Van Ban Schoten. It's such an unusual name, I thought it must be the same person, and sure enough I saw the adult Steven Van Ban Schoten perform on the stage. After the performance, I went backstage and reintroduced myself. He was delighted to see me and very quickly we started to talk about our grammar school. I said, "Didn't you think it was a spectacular place?" He said that he thought they did a great job teaching him how to write and read but admitted, "You know, they had very little in the performing arts, certainly very little in music. Did you know I even had to wait until the second grade to take piano lessons?" I confessed to him, "Steven, that was my fault. Sister Philip Neri was so sensitive to the fact that I had one arm that she said only the girls could take it my year." Steven looked at me very strangely, and I'm not certain that he believed me.

French Cream of Mushroom Soup

4 tablespoons butter or margarine
1 pound mushrooms, thinly sliced
2 shallots, finely chopped
1 tablespoon flour
½ teaspoon salt
½ teaspoon dried savory
Pinch of white pepper
2 teaspoons tomato paste
1 can beef broth
1 tablespoon lemon juice
2 cups half-and-half
2 tablespoons dry vermouth

MELT THE BUTTER in a 3-quart pan over moderately high heat. Add the mushrooms and shallots and cook, stirring often, until the mushrooms brown lightly and most of their liquid is gone.

Sprinkle with the flour, salt, savory, and pepper. Add the tomato paste. Stir the mushrooms to coat with the added ingredients. Remove from the heat and gradually blend in the beef broth. Bring to a boil, cover, reduce heat, and simmer for 20 minutes.

Puree the mushroom mixture in a blender or food processor until smooth, mixing in the lemon juice at the end. Return to the cooking pan, blend in half-and-half, and stir often over medium heat until steaming hot. Do not boil. Taste, and add salt if needed.

Add the vermouth and serve at once.

SERVES: 6

WHEN I WAS FIRST INTRODUCED to the Mexican author Laura Esquivel, I didn't realize who she was. After one of NTWH's performances, she told me she wanted to write on our behalf. "Are you a writer?" I queried. Much to my embarrassment, in her humility she simply answered "Yes." A fellow Jesuit whispered into my ear, "Dunderhead, she's the author and screenwriter of *Like Water for Chocolate*." We since have become great friends. She cooks for me often, and shows me the warmth and love of all of Mexico from her kitchen. This Sherried Black Bean Soup has a Mexican tang.

Sherried Black Bean Soup

1 pound dried black beans, rinsed and drained

8 cups water

2 tablespoons butter or margarine

2 medium onions, chopped

1 stalk celery, thinly sliced

1 medium carrot, shredded

1 clove garlic, minced or pressed

1 ham hock (about 1 pound)

¼ cup chopped fresh parsley

1 teaspoon salt

⅛ teaspoon cayenne pepper

⅛ teaspoon whole cloves

⅛ teaspoon mustard seed

1 bay leaf

⅓ cup dry sherry

Thinly sliced green onions, crumbled crisp bacon, sour cream, sieved,
*   hard-cooked egg, and thin lemon slices, for garnish*

IN A LARGE, heavy saucepan, bring the beans and 4 cups of water to a boil. Boil briskly for 2 minutes, then remove from the heat and let stand, covered, for 1 hour.

In a 5-quart Dutch oven, melt the butter. Add the onions, celery, carrot, and garlic, and cook until soft but not browned. Add the ham hock, the remaining 4 cups water, parsley, salt, cayenne pepper, cloves, mustard seed, bay leaf, and beans (with their liquid). Bring to a boil, cover, reduce heat, and simmer for about 3 hours.

Remove the ham hock and let cool slightly. Remove and discard bay leaf. Place about half of the beans with about 1 cup of the liquid from the soup in a blender or food processor. Process until smooth. Return the puree to the soup in the Dutch oven.

Remove the ham from its bone and add the meat to the soup. (Discard fat, bones, and skin.) Reheat the soup over medium heat. Stir in the sherry.

Serve hot soup with choice of garnishes to sprinkle on top.

SERVES: 8

HERMAN BRUELMAN IS A JESUIT whom I first met while we were in Cologne, Germany. He was stationed in Bonn, where he was in charge of a graduate center for Catholic students. One summer, they visited New York City on an exchange, and prior to the visit, he came to America House, where I was able to help arrange for their stay.

Herman and I became friends. It was astounding to listen to him describe the fall of the Berlin Wall. It was an event of great significance in his life, because he, in fact, was the first Jesuit from the West to take over a Jesuit high school that had been isolated in East Berlin during the Communist occupation. While visiting Herman in Bonn prior to his move to East Berlin, we went out to dinner together, and during that dinner, I said, "Herman, I really feel we're very good friends, but I don't know much about you." And he told me his remarkable story.

He said that he was born out of wedlock to a Jewish actress, and that his father married his mother while Herman was an infant. His father rescued him from the fate of his mother, who was exiled and gassed at Auschwitz. It wasn't until he was sixteen years old that Herman learned about his past. He was an adolescent, and in his distress, he consulted a Jesuit at the prep school he was attending. The Jesuit listened to Herman's account and said, "Ach, my heavens! Every step of the way you have been loved." And as far as Herman was concerned, that was the end of the story.

What a memorable evening that was for me. Here I was in a German restaurant listening to my Jesuit friend tell me a personal piece of his German history, while I was supping on French Onion Soup.

French Onion Soup

4 cups thinly sliced onions (about 1 pound)

1 teaspoon sugar

4 tablespoons butter and/or rendered chicken fat

1 tablespoon olive oil

2 cloves garlic, finely minced

2 tablespoons unbleached flour

¼ teaspoon dry mustard

¼ cup cognac, heated

2 cups dark beef stock

2 cups brown chicken stock

1¼ cups beef consommé

¼ teaspoon freshly grated nutmeg

⅛ teaspoon black pepper

½ teaspoon Worcestershire sauce

Salt to taste

½ cup dry vermouth or dry white wine

6 rusks or sourdough French bread slices, toasted

6 tablespoons each freshly grated Gruyère and Parmesan, or Comté or Beaufort, or crumbled Gorgonzola

BROWN THE ONIONS AND SUGAR in butter and oil. Add the garlic; cook for 3 minutes and sprinkle with the flour and mustard. Raise the heat and continue stirring for 3 minutes.

Pour the cognac over the mixture, ignite, and let burn down. Add the stocks, consommé, nutmeg, pepper, and Worcestershire sauce. Cover, bring to a boil, lower the heat and simmer for 20 minutes. Add salt as desired. Cool the soup and refrigerate it overnight in order to mellow the flavor. Reheat and adjust seasonings to taste. Add the vermouth before serving. Top the soup off with rusks or toast sprinkled with cheese.   *SERVES: 8*

ONE OF THE GREAT PASSIONS in my life is training persons with disabilities so that they can find work. For a number of years, I had been baking breads for our benefactors at both Christmas and Easter time. Our benefactors had really grown in numbers and I was going to need help if I wanted to get breads out in time for Christmas. I asked my students if any of them would like to volunteer to help me bake breads for our benefactors. Much to my surprise, nine students eagerly raised their hands to volunteer. By the time we set up a baking schedule, we had eleven volunteers, all of whom were disabled. In a very short time, we were able to produce some really beautiful loaves of Christmas bread to send to our benefactors.

It was really quite wonderful to be able to adapt the conditions in our small bakery creatively to meet the needs of the various disabilities. I've always believed that adaptability is one of the great uses of the imagination. I was delighted to see that our little people found easier access to the oven doors than those of us who were tall. Our blind students were more than capable of chopping nuts and vegetables on a cutting board. We were able to lower tables for some of our students and raise tables for others.

This was actually the reason that I went back to look at all the recipes I had gathered over the years from Jesuit Brothers, to see which kinds of breads I would like to continue to bake. I was so stunned by the number of recipes I had that I said to myself, either I have to throw these recipes out, or put them in some kind of order and write a cookbook. That was the inception of *The Secrets of Jesuit Breadmaking*.

After we began to bake bread, I arrived at the idea that certain students should be trained to become bakers, in the hope that they could supplement their income while they were becoming actors. Most actors in New York City supplement their income by being waiters and waitresses. Although I'm an extraordinary advocate for the rights of the disabled, I hardly think that waiting tables is the best idea for persons with disabilities.

After the book came out, I got a telephone call from a reporter for National Public Radio. He said that he had a copy of my book and would very much like to review it, but that he was also anxious to talk to me about the bakery we were running and the National Theatre Workshop of the Handicapped. He asked me what my schedule was like. I told him that we were knee-deep in preparing the St. Peter Canisius's Stollen for our benefactors in time for Christmas. I also told him that our Cabaret, the professional arm of NTWH, was rehearsing for the Christmas show and that this would be a good time for him to come along, in order to see our bakery as well as our Cabaret. He scheduled two days when he could bring his crew to record both events.

I had alerted all of our students in the bakery that we would be interviewed for a radio show. However, while we were waiting for his arrival, we were all very busy preparing the stollen. I was surprised to look up and find him standing there. This reporter seemed a very bright, and energetic, bald-headed fellow, but he seemed a little distracted. I later discovered that he had been greeted at our door by a blind woman carrying a large knife. But he seemed to show no powers of recovery whatsoever, and he really appeared quite uncomfortable with the disabled students in the bakery, spending most of the morning interviewing me as I supervised the making of the bread. Nevertheless, he made arrangements to return the next day with more sophisticated sound equipment so he could record some of the music that was being rehearsed by the Cabaret.

That night, I got out of bed and sat in my prayer chair. I know that when I have a headache, it means that I am angry at something, so I spent some time trying to figure out why I was angry. It became clear to me that the reason was because this perfectly fine man had brought some very negative feelings to our disabled students in the bakery that day. His discomfort was something the students were able to pick up on very quickly. Indeed, one of the little people was so annoyed by his not paying any attention to him that he actually walked between his legs.

The reporter arrived the next day with sound equipment to record the Cabaret, and dutifully listened to about an hour of the rehearsal. Afterward, he asked if he could interview some of the students. Now, the students who are in the Cabaret are our seasoned veterans. These students have worked professionally, and are much more articulate than most of our other students. He sat all of us down and started on a line of very negative questions. He asked, "Don't you feel badly that Broadway and Hollywood don't make a concerted effort to recruit you, as disabled persons, to be in movies and on stage?" He was also saying, "Don't you find it hard to be disabled?"— always along lines of negativity.

The interview was really going nowhere, although everyone was polite. Finally, he asked, "What annoys you?" and I immediately blurted out that what annoyed me were journalists who held negative attitudes toward the disabled. I said, "For the last two days you have done nothing but harp on the negative aspects of what it means to be disabled. Yesterday, you committed the unpardonable sin of ignoring them. Instead of looking around that bakery and seeing this miracle of persons with various disabling conditions all working together to create some wonderful gifts for our benefactors, in your discomfort you decided to ignore it and just concentrate on interviewing me." His bald head snapped back, and with his penetrating, intelligent eyes, he peered into the eyes of Sandy, a very attractive woman of color with leg braces, and said to her, "All right, Sandy, you said that you would like to play on a soap opera. What role could you possibly play?" Without missing a beat, she replied, "The bitch." That stopped him dead in his tracks. After he got his breath back, he turned to Bobbie, a woman in a wheelchair, who volunteered, "You told me that I couldn't play Broadway, because no Broadway theater has a ramp for a person in a wheelchair. But let me tell you something: if I get a role on Broadway, I'll get up on that stage every night, twice on Wednesdays, and twice on Saturdays, because that's my job."

He turned to me and said, "You know, Rick, of all the things that you've been saying about your wonderful organization, the thing that I find most offensive is that you refer to the disabilities as blessings." I told him, "You know, I'm fifty-three years old, and was born with one arm, but at this stage in my life I am happier to have one arm than to be bald."

Here's a classic beans and pork soup that works as a one-dish meal when served with bread.

White Bean and Smoked Pork Soup

3 tablespoons butter

½ pound slab bacon or any smoked pork, diced

3 large onions, sliced

1 clove garlic, minced

2 cups cooked white kidney beans

4 parsley sprigs

½ teaspoon dried thyme

½ teaspoon dried tarragon

1 bay leaf

Salt and pepper to taste

8 cups water

½ cup finely chopped parsley

MELT THE BUTTER IN A KETTLE and sauté the bacon until it is golden and crisp. Add the onions and cook for 5 minutes. Add the remaining ingredients except for chopped parsley, cover, and cook over low flame for 15 minutes. Remove the bay leaf and sprigs of parsley and sprinkle in chopped parsley.

SERVES: 6 TO 8

Golden Squash Soup

This squash soup is a recipe given to me by my friend Sister Jo Anne Flora, S.N.D., who as a high school student attended Notre Dame Academy on Rittenhouse Square in Philadelphia together with my sister, Denise, who now is also a Sister of Notre Dame.

> *1 piece golden squash (about 1½ pounds)*
> *2 tablespoons butter or margarine*
> *1 small onion, finely chopped*
> *1 tablespoon flour*
> *2 tablespoons chunky peanut butter*
> *1 (14-ounce) can chicken broth*
> *½ teaspoon salt*
> *½ teaspoon dry mustard*
> *Pinch of white pepper*
> *Pinch of cayenne pepper*
> *2 cups milk*
> *Sour cream, for garnish*

PREHEAT OVEN to 400 degrees.

Place the squash cut side down in a greased baking dish, cover, and bake until very tender (40 to 50 minutes). Scoop out the squash and discard rind. (You should have approximately 2 cups cooked squash.) Puree in a blender or food processor, or press through a food mill.

Melt the butter in a 3-quart saucepan over medium heat. Add the onion and cook until soft but not browned. Blend in the flour, then the peanut butter. Remove from the heat and gradually blend in the chicken broth.

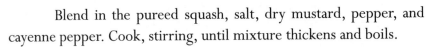

Blend in the pureed squash, salt, dry mustard, pepper, and cayenne pepper. Cook, stirring, until mixture thickens and boils.

Blend in the milk and heat to serving temperature. Serve topped with dollops of sour cream.

SERVES: 6

Lent

*L*ove consists in sharing what one has and

what one is with those one loves. Love ought to

show itself in deeds more than in words.

ST. IGNATIUS LOYOLA

I COULD HARDLY WAIT for my fourteenth birthday when I would be old enough to apply to the state of Pennsylvania for the working papers that would allow me to hold a job. In those days, getting working papers was a rite of passage for teenage independence. Almost immediately after my papers arrived from the State Department of Employment I landed a job as soda jerk at Eagle Drug, a neighborhood pharmacy owned and operated by Morris and Esther Bloomfield. Morris and his son Gene worked in the pharmacy department, while Esther, whom we called Mrs. Bloomfield, ran the soda fountain and candy stand. My duties included helping Mrs. Bloomfield dispense delicious ice cream delights at the soda fountain and delivering prescriptions by bicycle to local customers.

At the beginning of Lent, Mrs. Bloomfield volunteered the information that there would be a sharp decline in candy and ice cream sales, but only for about the first ten days of the season. She had noticed a lack of resolve on the part of our Catholic customers who had promised to refrain from eating sweets for the duration of Lent but who would gradually slip back onto their favorite soda fountain stools way before the forty days were over. This astute observation left a profound impression on me and I wondered why we did lose our resolve.

We all started out on Ash Wednesday with such great fervor that it seemed that nothing could frustrate our good intentions, but sure enough within about ten days our zeal was so diminished that infidelity to our Lenten resolutions became obvious even to an ice cream and candy vendor. Yet I should not have been surprised, because this familiar human trait is what the megabillion dollar diet industry relies on to keep its business flourishing.

Clearly this approach to Lent is not working. Sheer deprivation may not be the answer. Maybe we should ask ourselves the fundamental question of what the purpose of Lent is. Lent is a special season in the Church year when we are invited to prepare ourselves spiritually for the upcoming celebration of the Lord's passion, death, and resurrection at Easter. Perhaps we are approaching this whole Lent deprivation thing in the wrong manner. What are we looking for? Are we seeking to be deprived or are we hoping to be happy in a closer relationship with our God? Certainly we know what God wants.

At the beginning of each Lenten season during my years at Wernersville our novice master cautioned us against excesses in fasting. He taught us that St. Ignatius wanted moderation in all things. Almighty God doesn't want our sacrifices: He wants our hearts. He wants us loving and contrite. He wants us to enjoy and revel in our relationship to Him.

The purpose of Lent is to bring us closer to God and any practice we perform during this sacred season should bring fulfillment and satisfaction with it, or we will truly lose our resolve.

The primary purpose of fasting is to condition our body to become more alert to God's proddings of love. But oftentimes the very act of fasting so distracts us from its original intent that it becomes a deterrent rather than a help.

What I often do in order to make those forty days leading up to Easter something positive is spend some time each day asking our Lord to show me the way to be happy through service to Him. I ask Him during that prayerful time to help me remember that we are all His beloved children, so that I can truly celebrate with those around me as a family in His glorious resurrection. Of course, I think there is no better way to celebrate "family" than by placing in front of your loved ones a steaming bowl of delicious homemade soup and thanking God both for them and for the soup. I find this is oftentimes a far more positive way to prepare for Easter Sunday than denying ourselves ice cream and candy at Eagle Drug Store.

IN THE EARLY 1970S, I was stationed at St. Joseph's University in Philadelphia. I was living in a residence hall with the students while attending Villanova University for a master's degree in theater. Religious life seemed at that time to be very turbulent, and a group of us thought that the only answer was a small community in which we would share all of the household chores, including cooking. We came together nightly to pray and cook with each other. We each took different nights to cook and quickly we learned which nights we could look forward to. I was the only brother in this small community, and my star quickly rose because I was the only one trained as a cook. My soups and breads became very popular. We were very anxious to make this small community successful, so this was not the time to experiment. One consistent crowd-pleaser was Minestrone Milanese, which I made on weekends. I then refrigerated it, and added the final touches on the night during the week that I served it. During Lent, you can omit or retain the meat portions of this recipe. The soup will be just as good.

Minestrone Milanese

1 cup dried cannellini or Great Northern beans, rinsed and drained

1 teaspoon salt

10 to 12 cups water

2 tablespoons olive oil

2½ to 3 pounds beef shanks, sliced ¾ to 1 inch thick

2 large onions, slivered

2 large carrots, chopped

2 stalks celery, thinly sliced

2 cloves garlic, minced or pressed

½ cup chopped parsley

1 smoked ham hock (about ¾ pound)

1 (28-ounce) can tomatoes, with their liquid, coarsely chopped

2 tablespoons dried basil

1 medium turnip, peeled and diced

2 cups chopped chard leaves

½ cup shelled fresh or frozen peas

1½ cups hot cooked rice

2 cups shredded cabbage

Salt to taste

Grated Parmesan cheese

PLACE THE BEANS in a large bowl; add 1 teaspoon salt and 2 cups water. Cover and let stand for at least 8 hours; drain, discarding soaking liquid. Or to shorten the soaking period, place the beans in a 2- to 3-quart pan with 4 cups water (no salt); bring to a boil, then boil briskly, uncovered, for 2 minutes. Remove from the heat, cover, and let stand for 1 hour. Drain, discarding soaking liquid.

In a 7- to 8-quart kettle, heat the olive oil over medium heat. Add the beef shanks and brown on all sides. As you turn the shanks to brown the last side, add the onions. Cook, stirring occasionally, until the onions are limp.

Add the carrots, celery, garlic, parsley, ham hock, tomatoes and their liquid, basil, drained, soaked beans, and 8 cups of the water. Bring to a boil, cover, and reduce heat. Simmer until the meats and beans are tender (3½ to 4 hours). Skim and discard surface fat if necessary.

Remove the beef shanks and ham hock with a slotted spoon. When cool enough to handle, discard bones and skin. Return beef and ham in large chunks to soup. (At this point, soup may be covered and refrigerated until ready to reheat and serve; skim fat from the surface before reheating.)

Add the turnip to the soup and boil gently, uncovered, for 10 minutes. Mix in the chard and peas and cook for 3 minutes more. Blend in the rice and cabbage and cook, stirring occasionally, just until cabbage is wilted and bright green (3 to 5 minutes). Taste, and add salt if needed.

Serve with Parmesan cheese to sprinkle over each serving.

SERVES: 6 TO 8

IGNATIUS LOYOLA WAS AGAINST severe fasting and asceticism. His proscription was the result of experience, because
after his conversion, he went through a period in which he did
great damage to his body by fasting and other penance. "Moderation in all things" became Ignatius's watchword. As novices,
we were introduced to a rather rigorous life of awakening at
5:30 in the morning, but also a very wise bedtime of 9:30 in
the evening, allowing growing young boys plenty of time to
sleep. Also, two weeks every summer, as well as Thursday and
a half day on Sunday every week, were designated as vacation
days, what we called Villa days. The two-week Villa in June was
an absolutely marvelous time. We finally had the chance to
hike the beautiful countryside surrounding Wernersville, Pennsylvania—to take bike trips, play tennis, go swimming, have
wonderful cookouts, and basically just enjoy all the good
things that such a beautiful area of the country provides. We
were able to read books that were not normally part of our
reading list. Moreover, it gave us a great opportunity for
camaraderie, as we were even able to put on a small play together. The whole idea was for us, in a very monitored and
guided situation, to learn how to relax. Prior to our first Villa,
our novice master said, "Remember: This is a vacation, but
there is never a vacation from God." And, in fact, what we
were learning was how to relax and enjoy the space that God
had so graciously given us.

On one of the Villa days, I arranged with two of my
fellow novices to take a bike ride. It was a rather simple affair,

and we were able to pack a small lunch that we fastened to the backs of the bikes. I can remember that one thin dime was Scotch-taped under the bikes. This was in keeping with our vows of poverty, as we were not carrying any money of our own; however, in case of an accident, we still had that one dime to make the all-important telephone call. So the two novices and I went off to the West Reading Art Museum, which was about a fifteen-mile bike ride. The museum, surprisingly enough, was filled with some absolutely beautiful art treasures, but, beyond that, the museum itself was in an absolutely gorgeous setting, near a pond with small waterfalls in a beautifully landscaped area. We arrived there around noon, the traditional time that we made our midday Examen of Conscience. The three of us thought it best to do that right then. The senior of our band was able to carry a watch, so he would let us know when the fifteen minutes were up. I found a beautiful park bench—the perfect spot to be alone and offer up my prayer. Sitting down to begin the Examen, I got about five minutes into my prayer, when a rather attractive young woman came up and sat down next to me. Perhaps she thought it strange that I wasn't lifting up my eyes to acknowledge her, but I did kind of nod very nicely as she sat down next to me and opened her box lunch. I guess she felt that she really should share, so right in the middle of my prayer, I saw an apple waved before my face, as if she were offering it to me. Images of Eve offering me the apple could not help but spring to mind, but because I didn't want to break my concentration in prayer, I just smiled and thanked her. We had such a myopic sense of what it meant to be novices that the thought of having our prayer interrupted by anyone was really anathema to us, and I handled it like a spartan monk rather than a more gracious human being. When the fifteen minutes were up, the novice who maintained the watch decided to let me know by giving me the normal salutation at the end of prayer, when we could break our silence and speak. He yelled across the pond, "Brother Curry, Brother Curry, praise be Jesus Christ," and I yelled back, "Forever, forever." And with that, the lady threw all of her food into her little parcel, got up, and walked briskly away. She must have thought I was some sort of religious lunatic.

Winter Squash Soup

4 tablespoons butter

2 medium onions, chopped fine

4 tablespoons flour

Generous grating of nutmeg

*2 cups homemade chicken stock or 2 cups water to which 3 chicken
    bouillon cubes, crushed, have been added*

4 cups milk

*2 (10-ounce) packages frozen winter squash, fully thawed to room
    temperature*

Salt to taste

White pepper to taste

Finely chopped parsley, for garnish

HEAT THE BUTTER in a large saucepan and cook the onions until translucent. Stir in the flour, and cook the mixture over gentle heat for a few minutes. Stir in the nutmeg.

Gradually add the stock and then the milk, stirring until the mixture is thickened and smooth.

Add the squash and simmer over moderate heat, covered, for 10 minutes. Season to taste with salt and pepper. Serve garnished with parsley.

SERVES: 6

I HAVE ALWAYS BEEN FASCINATED with French cooking and cuisine and secretly thought that being a French Jesuit must be heaven. The Custom Book adjusted the universal regulations of the Society of Jesus to particular countries or provinces and would be a great source for learning how my brothers in France dined. A friend of mine, Dennis Michael Linehan, S.J., researched the Custom Books of France in the 1880s. Given the French interest in cuisine, and our interest in the bourgeois table of the nineteenth century, we might expect considerable attention to be given to food and drink, and Dennis was not disappointed in what he found.

He told me that breakfast was normally slight, little more than bread and milk; and the noon meal was ample, with supper often a matter of leftovers. A Jesuit would enter the refectory for the noon meal, take his napkin from a numbered box, and proceed to table to wait for the Latin grace to be recited in common. If, however, he was the superior or the provincial, his napkin would already be at his assigned place. Fixed places were designated only for superiors, or visitors, who sat beside the superior. In his absence, the superior's place was vacant. At each place, there were two plates, a glass, a knife, a fork, and a spoon. Three serving spoons and four serving forks were placed in the middle of the table, along with a full plate of bread, a pitcher of water, and a condiment plate of salt, pepper, vinegar, and olive oil. Each course was to be served individually, with the exception of vegetables, butter, cheese, and wine. In the France Province, mention is made of the permitted substitution of beer or cider according to the custom, testimony to the presence of Alsatians, Lorrainers, Bretons, and Normans. The Custom Book of the Lyon Province made no mention of this deviation. The main meal was at noon: it was substantial. On ordinary days, the meal would begin with bouillon, followed by a substantial soup, then a meat course with vegetables. The dessert was fruit and cheese. When cheese was served in the France Province, it was customary to put it on the table for each to serve himself as he wished. Butter could substitute for cheese, according to regional custom.

When I visited the Paris Jesuit Community in 1968 at the Rue de Grenelle, this is the soup that they served at the noon meal. All my fantasies about the French Jesuits and their dining became a reality and I was not disappointed. However, it was very difficult for me to arm-wrestle the recipe away from the brother cook. French chefs are known to keep their recipes secret.

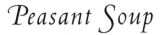

Peasant Soup

½ pound salt pork

10 cups water

1 pound broccoli, washed and cut into 1-inch pieces

2 potatoes, peeled and diced

2 cloves garlic, minced

Salt and pepper to taste

1 teaspoon heavy cream

1 teaspoon sour cream

8 slices French bread, toasted in oven

IN COLD WATER, soak the pork overnight, or for 6 to 8 hours. Rinse under running cold water. Remove and discard the rind. Cube the pork into pieces of approximately ½ inch. Put the diced pork into a kettle, then add the water. Cover and cook over medium heat for 1 hour. Add the broccoli, potatoes, garlic, salt, and pepper and cook together for 25 minutes. Mix the heavy cream and sour cream in a bowl, dilute with some of the soup, and then stir into the kettle.

Pour the soup over toasted bread slices when serving.

SERVES: 6 TO 8

OUR LIVES ARE FILLED with rituals that we often don't reflect upon. There was a ritual on Sundays that had become a fixture in my life, and I hardly reflected on it until I began to write this book. Sunday morning, I would gather at America House for Mass with the community there, where the principal celebrant is usually John W. Donohue, S.J., one of the editors of *America* magazine. John and I have been friends for many years, ever since I lived in the actual community at America House, and he is now in his eighties. This has not stopped him from being vigorous in both mind and body. He begins every homily by saying that he is not going to preach a homily, and certainly not a sermon, and he gives various reasons as to why. Instead, he says that he has three points. Every one of his audio missives to us is delivered in three points. I always try to remember all the wonderful things that he's said, but one Sunday in particular stands out. It really is amazing to me that I have not forgotten what he said about "doing the next right thing."

The little theology goes like this: often in this very confusing world, we can get lost, and distracted from how we should live. What we are searching for seems to be in such compliance with the Gospels and so readily available; simply, we should do the next right thing. We generally know what that is. When I questioned Father Donohue further about this theology, he told me that the great exponent of this position was Jean-Pierre de Caussade, S.J. (1675–1751), in *The Sacrament of the Present Moment*. After Caussade's death, a treatise entitled *Self-Abandonment to Divine Providence* was compiled from conferences he had given to Visitation Nuns. In it, Caussade argues persuasively that Christians can always tell what they should be doing, at least in the here-and-now. This entails the fulfillment of God's will, since God only requires that we accomplish as well as possible the work of the present moment, and faithfully accept those demands with their own satisfactions or stifling limitations. Fix your attention successively, Caussade said, on the duty of each moment, like the hour hand of a clock that minute by minute moves the necessary distance. "God reveals Himself to little ones in the smallest things; while the great, who in their own conceit get no farther than the outer rings of events, do not find Him in even greater things." This is so compatible with Ignatius Loyola, asking us to find God's presence in the world in the simplest things. I have grown to be convinced that divine action and grace can be discovered precisely in all that happens to and around us.

After these delightful Sunday liturgies, we as a community would go into the kitchen and forage through the refrigerators, either making tuna salad or trying to reheat some wonderful soup like the following.

French Vegetable Soup

½ pound salt pork, diced

1 onion, minced

3 carrots, peeled and sliced

3 potatoes, peeled and cubed

1 celery stalk, diced

1 turnip, peeled and cubed

1 cup finely chopped parsley

3 quarts water

Pepper and salt to taste

8 slices French bread

4 tablespoons butter

SAUTÉ THE PORK IN A SKILLET until it is translucent. Add the onion and cook over low flame until it, too, is translucent (make sure that it is not brown). Add the remaining ingredients except for the bread and butter.

Cover with water, or meat stock if at all possible, bring to a boil, and let simmer for 15 minutes. Once the vegetables are tender, the soup is ready.

Sauté the bread slices in butter. Then, dice them into croutons and sprinkle a few on top of each dish of soup.

SERVES: 8 TO 10

WHEN I WAS SIX YEARS OLD, my sister, Denise, who was eight at the time, came across a comic book about Peter Gray. Pete Gray was a professional baseball player who had one arm. She learned from the book how he could catch a ball and throw it back using just his one hand. She took me out in the backyard, where we would practice for hours. I would catch the ball in my glove, throw the ball up into the air, with the stump of my right arm grab the glove off my left hand, catch the ball with my left hand, and throw it back. With what seemed like endless hours of practice, I really got quite adept at this, even to a point that she said she thought I could play short-stop—although mostly we just played catch.

That summer, while down at our house on the south Jersey shore, a zealous father of one of my friends organized a baseball league. When it came time for me to bat, I realized that I didn't know much about batting, and I struck out. I dropped the bat to walk away from home plate, and the father said, "Wait a minute, wait a minute. He gets another chance. He gets *three* more chances." Well, his math was very good: if you had two hands, you got three outs, and if you had one hand, you got six outs. I didn't think this was such a bad deal, so I went back to pick up the bat.

My sister put her fingers in her mouth to blow her all-familiar whistle, and I turned my head at the sound and saw her waving for me to come off the baseball diamond—which I did, dropping the bat—and she declared, "We're going home."

And with that she said to the guy, "Sorry, mister, we have to be leaving."

I asked her, "Why are we going home?"

She said, "We're going home because you struck out. And you're allowed to strike out. You're allowed to strike out like anybody else. Don't let anyone tell you that you can't strike out."

That night at dinner my father asked how the baseball game had gone, and Denise said, "You know, Ricky doesn't much like playing baseball," which was absolutely true because I didn't like the heat of the hot sun. She said, "Ricky prefers the water." And that's also true. Since that day, I have had an incredible love affair with all things aquatic. And I have had equal enthusiasm for my sister, Denise, who really knew some of life's wisdom at a very early age.

Whenever I recall stories like this one from my early childhood, I always think of tomato soup with mushrooms. It was a favorite of my mother and has become for me the ultimate comfort food. Linking fond memories with favorite foods is a terrific combination for happiness.

Mushroom and Tomato Soup

1 package dried cèpes or other mushrooms, soaked in water to cover
*   for 10 minutes*
6 cups chicken stock
4 tomatoes, peeled and cubed
3 cloves garlic, minced
Juice of 1 lemon
1 cup heavy cream
2 egg yolks
½ cup finely chopped parsley
Salt and pepper to taste

DRAIN THE MUSHROOMS and discard the water. Mix the mushrooms, stock, tomatoes, garlic, and lemon juice in a kettle. Bring them to a boil, reduce the heat, cover, and simmer for 45 minutes.

Combine the cream and yolks in a cup. Turn off the heat. Stir in cream-egg mixture, parsley, salt, and pepper.

SERVES: 4 TO 6

My sister, Denise Curry, a sister of Notre Dame de Namur, was a very normal girl and I can remember her locking horns with my mother when she was a teenager. My mother used to tell the story of the day when Denise went off to school and my mother found a note under her pillow that said, "Be mad at Mom in the morning."

When Denise was a novice in the Sisters of Notre Dame de Namur, my brother Jack came with us to see her on one of the visiting days. My brother was then trying to sell his house. He said to Denise, "Denise, would you pray, and have your novices pray that I sell my house?"

With complete sincerity, Denise turned to him and said, "Jackie, we're not very good at real estate. We're very good on health. If you have any health problems, we'll guarantee you success with those prayers."

This following recipe is one of Denise's favorites.

Bean Sprout Soup

1 fowl, disjointed (about 5 pounds)
1 large onion, quartered
2 bay leaves
2 whole cloves
1 tablespoon sugar
1 teaspoon salt
3 tablespoons vegetable oil
3 medium onions, finely chopped
1½ cups bean sprouts (preferably fresh, but canned will do)
2 teaspoons ground ginger

ARRANGE THE FOWL, onion, bay leaves, cloves, sugar, and salt in a soup kettle, and cover with water by 1 inch. Bring to a boil, reduce the heat, and simmer the fowl, covered, for 1½ hours, until it is very tender.

Remove the chicken and strain the broth. Discard the bones and skin of the chicken and cut the meat into thin julienne. Return it to the broth. Allow the broth to cool, refrigerate overnight, and the following day remove any solidified fat.

Heat the oil in a skillet and cook the onions until they are golden. Add the bean sprouts and sprinkle ginger over. Cook, stirring, for 5 minutes. Add the sprout mixture to the reheated broth and cook for 10 minutes.

SERVES: 6

WHEN I WAS STATIONED back in Philadelphia in the late 1960s and early 1970s, I had a wonderful opportunity to become reacquainted with my family. My father called me occasionally, but my mother called me religiously once a week. On Sunday afternoons, I tried to make it a point to go over to their home and have Sunday dinner with them. Occasionally, I brought one or two of the college students who lived in the dorm with me. It was really quite a workout for my mother because she had forgotten how much young boys eat.

When I was leaving after one of these visits, my father pulled me aside and told me that something was upsetting him. His attorney, a lifelong friend of his, had suddenly passed away. My father had to get a new attorney, which was unsettling enough to him, but in the process of going over his finances, he discovered that my mother had her own small bank account. This disturbed him, because he thought this was information that he was not supposed to discover. Having tripped over it, he was a little surprised that she was keeping such a secret from him.

I tried to calm him down and let him know that all of us children knew that Mom had this small bank account. I reassured him, saying, "Dad, it's really just a more sophisticated version of an Irish woman's teakettle." Mom was too bright to keep her money in a teakettle, and therefore had kept some of her husband's money in a small local bank account. I had to wait until the following day, when my father was out of the house, to call my mother and see if this, in fact, had caused any family disturbance. I asked her, "Ma, are you all right?" She responded, "Why wouldn't I be all right?" I told her that Dad had discovered her secret bank account. "Oh," she said, "he found the smaller one. I have two of them, you know."

Escarole Soup

I received this recipe from a Sister who learned it from her mother, who in turn learned it from her mother, who came to America around 1890 from Castel-franco in Miscano, Italy.

1 head escarole
2 tablespoons finely chopped onion
2 tablespoons finely chopped carrot
2 tablespoons extra-virgin olive oil
1 clove garlic, minced
4 cups chicken broth
1 recipe small meatballs (recipe follows)
Salt and pepper to taste
Freshly grated Parmesan cheese

WASH THE ESCAROLE WELL. Cut off the coarse white part of the stems. Stack the tender green leaves and cut them into strips about ½ inch wide.

In a soup pot, sauté the onion and carrot in the olive oil over medium heat for about 2 minutes. Add the garlic and sauté for about 1 minute more. Add the escarole and chicken broth and bring to a boil. Add the meatballs and simmer, covered, on low heat for about 15 minutes. Add salt and pepper to taste.

Serve steaming hot with a generous sprinkling of freshly grated Parmesan cheese and a thick slice of crusty Italian bread.

SERVES: 4

Meatballs

1 inch pile of bread—about three slices

1½ pounds of ground meat

    ½ pound beef

    ½ pound veal

    ½ pound pork

    or any other combination you like

2 eggs

1 tablespoon butter

¼ cup minced onion

3 tablespoons chopped fresh parsley

1¼ teaspoons salt

¼ teaspoon paprika

½ teaspoon grated lemon rind

1 teaspoon lemon juice

1 teaspoon Worcestershire sauce

SOAK THE BREAD IN WATER. Mix the meat together in a bowl. Add the eggs, well-beaten, and set the meat and egg mixture aside. Melt the butter in a frying pan and sauté onions until brown. Add sautéed onions to meat mixture. Wring out the bread, pull it apart, and mix it in with the meat. Add parsley, salt, paprika, lemon rind and juice, and Worcestershire sauce. Form into little balls.

STANISLAUS KOSTKA WAS ONLY EIGHTEEN when he died, and he had been a Jesuit novice for only one year. Naturally, therefore, he is the patron saint of all novices. His feast day is November 13. Stanislaus, born into an upper-class family, was fourteen when his father enrolled him and his brother Paul in a Jesuit college in Vienna, where they lived in rooms rented from a senator. Stanislaus was serious and prayerful, while Paul caroused tirelessly. Paul would often harass his brother about his devotion, and occasionally became violent.

I was assigned to read a book about Stanislaus while I was in the novitiate, and in the style of modern hagiography, it was entitled *Stanley Pole*. I read this book seriously during *Vita Sancti,* a half-hour period set aside for reading biographies of saints. After I completed it, I discussed it with my novice master. I was eighteen myself at the time, and in a light moment said that I sometimes found his drunken brother Paul much more attractive than the perpetually somber Stanislaus. My novice master did not laugh, and asserted instead that I had missed the point. As a result, he ordered me to reread the book. Over the years, I have gained a deeper appreciation for Stanislaus and his home country. When I arrived in New York City, St. Peter's Cathedral had an altar devoted to Stanislaus, and a statue depicting him. At one point, both altar and statue inexplicably disappeared. When the announcement was made that the Polish Karol Wojtýla was elected Pope John Paul II, the altar and statue reappeared overnight.

This most unusual dill pickle soup was talked about for years by Brother Biniakiewicz, who was a delightful old brother who worked with me in the tailor shop at the novitiate. Although he was born in Posen, Germany, and came to Buffalo at the age of four, he was always talking about Polish food. It was years after Brother Benny's death that I came across this recipe, and every time I serve this soup, I tell my guests about this Santa Claus-like Jesuit and what a powerful effect his charm and zeal had on my life.

Dill Pickle Soup

6 medium dill pickles, diced and drained on absorbent paper
4 tablespoons flour
4 tablespoons butter
5 cups homemade chicken stock or 4 (10½-ounce) cans chicken
  broth
½ teaspoon pepper
2 cups sour cream
Salt
½ cup finely chopped parsley, for garnish

COMBINE THE DICED PICKLES and flour in a paper bag; while holding the bag closed, shake vigorously.

Heat the butter in a large saucepan and cook the pickles, stirring, for 5 minutes. Add the stock and pepper. Bring the liquid to a boil, reduce the heat, and simmer, covered, for 30 minutes. Add the sour cream to the liquid, using a wire whisk to blend well.

Bring the soup to serving temperature. Add salt to taste. Serve garnished with parsley.

SERVES: 6

IN THE PRE–VATICAN II NOVITIATE, the dinner hour on certain evenings was known as a "penance night." There was an entire ritual surrounding this penance night. You could never perform a penance without getting permission to do so. That reflected a strong Ignatian principle in regard to the direction of one's soul. You were always to submit to the wisdom of others before you practiced an extraordinary penance. Therefore, you needed the permission of the minister—the official who supervised the temporal affairs of the house—before you performed one of the traditional penance rituals on entering the dining room.

There was a penance table known as *mensa,* the simple Latin word for table, where you could take your meal kneeling. Another form of penance was called *manes,* meaning hands. To take this penance, you extended your hands as you walked into the dining room. If the minister nodded, you knelt down and extended your arms during the graces. You would make the humble gesture, which meant that, remaining on your knees, you bent down and kissed the floor before rising and sitting down.

Another form of penance was *pedes,* which meant that after the recitation of the graces, you pulled your chair away, got down on your knees, and kissed the tips of the shoes of the brethren who were seated around you. You got permission to take *pedes* by approaching the minister, and taking your napkin out of the napkin box and kissing it. If he nodded, you had permission.

Needless to say, as young men of eighteen to twenty, we found all of this extraordinary form of penance quite enjoyable, and rather exciting. The practice could produce some unintentional humor. There was, for instance, the evening when one of the novices had fresh polish on the tips of his shoes. When another novice went underneath the table to kiss those shoes, he came back up with black lips. Peals of laughter sometimes would erupt around the refectory as we would joyfully dig into a meatless soup "celebrating" our penance night.

Zucchini Soup

1 tablespoon butter

1 small onion, chopped

3 large zucchini, seeded and cut in ½-inch pieces

1 bay leaf

3 sprigs of parsley

½ teaspoon thyme

*6 cups vegetable stock or 6 cups water plus envelopes vegetable
bouillon powder*

2 eggs, beaten

Generous grating of nutmeg

Salt and pepper to taste

HEAT THE BUTTER in a large saucepan and cook the onion until translucent. Add the zucchini, bay leaf, parsley, thyme, and stock. Bring to a boil, reduce the heat, and simmer, uncovered, for 10 minutes. Discard the bay leaf and parsley.

Whisk 1 cup of the broth into the beaten eggs. Add this mixture to the soup, stirring vigorously. Season to taste with nutmeg, salt, and pepper.

SERVES: 6 TO 8

AT THE NOVITIATE IN WERNERSVILLE, the refectory was filled with long, rectangular tables in the monastic style. The plates, the glasses, the china, the silverware, were all from military sources. Indeed, the china was composed of rejections from the United States Navy. The cups were white porcelain, and very heavy and very large. I remember on my first morning in the novitiate, lifting the coffee cup up to my lips, realizing how heavy it was, and how my wrist needed support to bring that cup to my lips. As the days and weeks and months went by, I became very familiar with this heavy crockery.

After six years in the Jesuits, I had a chance for a home visit that would last about two hours. I was on my way to another mission, and I was able to surprise my mother and father by an afternoon visit. I thought it would be a great delight to go to our front door (which was rarely used) and ring the doorbell to surprise my mother. It was a different era. We never had a key to our front door because we never had to lock it. I rang the doorbell, and sure enough the door opened.

It was the middle of winter, and my mother showed such great surprise to see me, she looked me up and down and said not "Hello," "How are you?," "Welcome home!," or any of those usual familial greetings, but rather "Where's your hat?"

And as naturally as if I had just stepped outside to play a game of handball, we sat down as we had always done at our kitchen table. My mother asked, "How about a cup of tea?" I said, "Great." I noticed that she went into the dining room to get the finest china, a real tribute to my return home. She brewed the tea in the teapot and poured me a cup, and as I reached over to pick it up, I nearly threw it right over my head, the cup was so light and the china so delicate. The rest of the two hours were spent in a bit of nervousness, actually, because my home seemed so fragile; after having lived in an institution for all of those years, I felt like a bull in a china shop. Everything seemed to be much smaller than I had remembered it. Then I realized that for the last six years of my life, I had been drinking coffee and tea in a dining room that was the size of an airplane hangar, hardly the size of our family kitchen. Yet the warmth and the companionship of my mother made it feel all so comfortable once again.

This soup will comfort you as well.

Chickpea and Vegetable Soup

2 unsalted pig's feet

4 quarts water

1 cup dried chickpeas, soaked overnight and drained

¼ pound cured ham, diced

2 tablespoons olive oil

1 medium onion, chopped

1 small green bell pepper, seeded and chopped

1 (6-ounce) can tomato paste

1 ½ teaspoons dried cilantro

½ cabbage, cored and shredded

3 medium potatoes, peeled and diced

½ pound pumpkin, pared and chopped

Salt and pepper to taste

COMBINE THE PIG'S FEET and water in a kettle, and boil, uncovered, for 1 ½ hours. Add the chickpeas, ham, olive oil, onion, green bell pepper, tomato paste, and cilantro. Simmer, covered, for 1 hour.

Add the cabbage, potatoes, and pumpkin and continue simmering for 45 minutes.

Uncover the kettle for the last 30 minutes so that the soup will thicken somewhat. Season to taste with salt and pepper.

SERVES: 6

When I was a freshman in high school at St. Joseph's Prep, I was totally enthusiastic and thought that I'd become a cheerleader. I went to the cheerleading audition and met the captain of the cheerleading squad, a young man named Joe Lacey, who would later become a Jesuit and a wonderful missionary to India, and who is now stationed in Washington, D.C. We were going to audition for the coveted two positions on the squad by doing a cheer called the locomotive, in which you got down on one knee and moved your forearm back and forth like a locomotive, saying, "SJP rah! SJP rah!" faster and faster. When Joe told every candidate to get down on his right knee and extend his left forearm, the cocaptain said, "Wait a minute, Joe, I thought we got down on our left knee and extended our right forearm." And Joe very wisely and kindly looked into his eyes and said, "Not this year." I don't have a right forearm, so Joe wanted to give me an equal chance at making the cheerleaders. I made the cheerleaders, but more than that, I've never forgotten the kindness of this extraordinary young man who has become an even more extraordinary Jesuit.

Lima Bean Soup

1 pound meaty beef bones, fat removed
1 large carrot, scraped and sliced
1 medium onion, chopped
½ cup chopped parsley leaves
1 (1-pound) can tomatoes, with their liquid
6 cups water
1½ cups shelled lima beans or 1 (10-ounce) package frozen lima
   beans
4 tablespoons cornstarch
⅓ cup milk
Salt and pepper to taste

COMBINE THE BEEF BONES, carrot, onion, parsley leaves, tomatoes, and water in a kettle. Bring to a boil, reduce the heat, and simmer, covered, for 2 hours, until the meat falls from the bones. Skim the surface with a slotted spoon as required.

Remove the meat and bones from the kettle. Chop the meat and reserve. Discard the bones. Refrigerate the broth and the reserved meat overnight, and the following day remove any solidified fat.

Bring the broth to a boil, add the lima beans, and cook, covered, for 25 minutes, until the beans are tender.

Blend together the cornstarch and milk in a small mixing bowl. Add this mixture to the broth, stirring until the soup is thickened and smooth. Stir in the reserved meat. Season to taste with salt and pepper.

SERVES: 6

THE YEAR WAS 1590, and the place was England. A woman named Ann Vaux found that it was necessary for her to secure a dwelling place that would be useful to the Jesuits during their yearly Manifestation of Conscience, the annual reckoning with their superiors. There was great danger in gathering Jesuits together during these years, when British Jesuits were persecuted for their faith. Baddesley Clinton was a secluded early Tudor mansion with a moat, set amid woods about a hundred miles from London. It was the perfect house for the purposes of retreat, and Ann immediately set about having the talented Jesuit Brother Nicholas Owen devise enough hiding places to conceal twelve or more Jesuit priests. This master carpenter, by using the moat and the levels of the sewer, together with secret turrets, trapdoors, and stairways, was able to ensure that Father Garnet and others survived the notorious search of 1591. These priests stood for four hours, half-immersed in water, but they were not captured. Brother Owen, a little man with a limp, had really not attracted much attention. After my years of working with the National Theatre Workshop of the Handicapped, I am familiar enough with the history of discrimination to know that a crooked body is often believed to denote a similarly twisted nature. Yet the great soul and measureless courage of Nicholas Owen, S.J., provide the strongest possible refutation of that silly, contemporary prejudice. This inconspicuous Jesuit brother, not much taller than a dwarf, actually held all the vital secrets of the Catholic hiding places in his craftsman's hands.

One of four sons of an Oxford carpenter, Brother Owen was nicknamed "Little John." Two of his brothers, Walter and John, were Jesuit priests. A third brother, Henry, ran a clandestine press for Catholic literature in Northamptonshire. Its publications were falsely stamped "Printed in Antwerp." At one point, after he was convicted for recusancy, Henry even set up a secret press in prison. In 1599, Little John—Brother Nicholas Owen—suffered an accident that crippled him, giving him a further disability beyond his small stature. A packhorse fell on top of him, severely damaging his leg. Poor setting of the bone did the rest. But when it came to working in the cramped conditions needed to construct a hiding place, such as a chimney or a drain, Little John's tiny size was a positive asset.

He nearly always worked alone, praying silently as he toiled away in the covering darkness of the night hours. Solitude was Little John's deliberate choice: he wanted no one else to share the danger at that time, or the threat of interrogation, including torture, afterward. Since Little John was among those who had been tortured in a London prison in 1594, hung up for three hours on end with his arms pinioned in iron rings and his body distended, he knew exactly the risks that he was taking. He probably worked for the Jesuit priest Edmund Campion, S.J., in the 1580s, and was certainly imprisoned for championing him in 1585. In 1586, however, he joined Father Garnet, and thenceforth accorded him his complete devotion. "How many Jesuits, then, do we think that this man saved?" contemplated Father Garnet rhetorically. For his part, Father Garnet described how Little John traveled all over the country, constructing hiding places for the Jesuits, priests, and other Catholics, so that they could conceal themselves from the fury of Protestant searchers. Yet, despite all the risks involved, Brother Owen did his chosen work free of charge. If any money was forced upon him, he gave it to his Brothers.

Working in the great thickness of Tudor masonry, a problem in itself, Little John had nevertheless to make a solid construction of his own, lest the taps of the searchers be met with a hollow report. It was also dangerous to use the space provided by chimneys, as fires might be set by the searchers. It was essential that each hiding place be different, lest the uncovering of one should lead to the uncovering of many others. Despite that danger, Brother Owen developed certain trademarks. In preparation for the long sojourn of many Jesuits, he passed feeding tubes or communication devices into the hiding places, and worked out a trick by which an outer hiding place concealed an inner one, in order to elude the searchers. These trademarks help to establish which hiding places in England are the works of Brother Owen. In addition to Baddesley Clinton, secret annexes at Saston Hall, near Cambridge, and Huntington Court, are generally rated as his work. Owen was probably responsible for the surviving hiding places at Coughton and Coldhan Halls. Coldhan Hall is still in private hands, and although considerably altered since the Rockwood days, nevertheless contains three hiding places constructed by Brother Owen. An added room, which was a chapel, is also extant. Little John found his vocation in the combined role of architect, mason, and carpenter of the numerous hiding places. His various constructions have been described as wordless prayers.

Spinach Soup

2 (10-ounce) packages fresh spinach, rinsed and shaken dry, the
    woody stems removed, or 2 (10-ounce) packages frozen chopped
    spinach, fully thawed to room temperature
5 cups water
1½ teaspoons salt
¼ teaspoon pepper
⅓ cup strained lemon juice
2 eggs, well beaten
Sour cream, for garnish, optional

COMBINE THE SPINACH, water, salt, and pepper in a large
saucepan. Bring to a boil, reduce the heat, and simmer for 12 minutes.
Allow the broth to cool.

Blend it, 2 cupfuls at a time, in a food processor. Return it to
the saucepan, along with the lemon juice and eggs. Warm the soup
over gentle heat.

If desired, garnish each serving with 1 tablespoonful of sour
cream.

SERVES: 6

IGNATIUS LOYOLA FOUGHT VERY HARD to establish a religious community of men who would not be bound by the recitation of the office in common, as the monks had been of old. Ignatius wanted his men to be out and about, and not restricted by going to chapel at least five times during the day. What he achieved was a kind of religious order that we are now comfortably calling an active religious community. As the years went by, however, certain monastic practices crept into Our lives, particularly in regard to formation, and one of them was known as the penance table. I described these penance practices earlier in the book, but let me say a bit more about the penance table.

Certain times of the year, but particularly during Advent and Lent, the chairs were removed from the sides of one table so that the novices or juniors could voluntarily take their meals kneeling down. The first time that I tried this form of penance, I was amazed to find that when you knelt on the floor, you were approximately at the same height as you would be when sitting on a chair. It wasn't as if your chin were resting on top of the table. Also, there were a few little perks to kneeling at the penance table: the servers were usually very sympathetic toward those of us around that table, and actually gave us a greater quantity and variety of food.

A hearty but meatless soup is the Vichyssoise.

Vichyssoise

5 medium leeks
2 tablespoons butter
1 small onion, finely chopped
3 medium smooth-skinned potatoes, peeled and diced
2 teaspoons salt
⅛ teaspoon white pepper
4 cups boiling water
1 cup milk
2 cups half-and-half
1 cup cold heavy cream
Salt to taste
Fresh chives, for garnish

CUT OFF THE ROOT ENDS and tops of the leeks. Wash, drain, and slice them about ¼ inch thick.

In a 3- to 4-quart saucepan over medium heat, melt the butter. Add the leeks and onion and cook, stirring often, until soft but not browned. Mix in the potatoes, salt, pepper, and the boiling water. Bring to a boil, cover, reduce heat slightly, and cook until the potatoes are very tender, 25 to 30 minutes.

Puree the mixture, about half at a time, in a blender or food processor until smooth. Return to the cooking pan. Blend in the milk and half-and-half. Stir over medium heat until steaming hot. Strain into a large bowl. Cover and refrigerate 3 to 5 hours or overnight.

Using a whisk, blend in the cream. Taste, and add salt if needed. Serve sprinkled with chives.

SERVES: 6 TO 8

A NUMBER OF YEARS AGO, I was lucky enough to be able to take a four-month sabbatical from my work in New York City with the National Theatre Workshop of the Handicapped. I went to Maine—more to restore my energy than for any particular work. I was at a very low point in my life, and was beginning to lose the drive for the work I had been doing. Burnout is insidious. It is a lot like walking pneumonia: you don't feel great, but you don't know how sick you really are. I was blessed to be able to talk to a great Jesuit friend of mine, and during the course of the conversation, he looked right at me and said, "Rick, you're tired. You're very tired. You have to get away." I told him I was thinking of going away for the weekend. He said, "I was thinking of your going away for a year. I think it's that desperate."

He got my attention. I began to look into possibilities for my getting away without doing grave harm to the work that I had been doing at the National Theatre Workshop of the Handicapped. I know that no one is indispensable but, at the same time, having begun this work and being the sole fundraiser for it, I thought that to move away from it for a year would really jeopardize its future. To this day, I believe that is true. But thanks to a very generous staff that was willing to go it alone for the duration of my sabbatical, I was able to break away for four months.

Now the question was, where would I go, and what would I do? I had been involved in basket making for a long time and had studied under an expert Shaker basket maker named John McGuire. I called to ask for his advice, and he said, "You should go to Haystack School of Crafts in Maine and study some more basket making up there. I think it would expand your horizons in regards to crafts." At his recommendation, I contacted Haystack School of Crafts in Deer Isle, Maine, and went up to explore the place. I found the school to be in an extraordinarily beautiful location on the coast of Maine, a place where I would not only enjoy learning some new crafts, but also be able to rest and restore my soul. There was a small cabin on the water that I was able to rent, and I arrived in springtime to begin my blessed sabbatical.

To my disappointment, the course at Haystack was led by a teacher who was somewhat offended by my impudence in presuming that I could do his intricate work in basket weaving with just one hand. And it was a struggle, I must admit, but it was something that I was willing to learn, and trying to conquer. Every time I would work on it, he would come up behind me, look at my basket, and say, "You can't do this. You can't do this." Such a refrain was very foreign to my ears growing up, because my parents had always encouraged me to try different things. They weren't unrealistic, but they taught me to explore all of my options, and I think that's also a particular trait of Jesuit education—that there's more than one way of doing something. I got the idea that if I could bend the rattan over a soccer ball and grab it with my small arm, that I could succeed, so I drove into town to find a sporting goods store. I found a soccer ball and thought, Yes, this could work, this could be adaptable to my technique. Then I saw the price of the ball, and was astounded by how expensive it was. I stopped suddenly and realized that I shouldn't have to accommodate this teacher, and I said to myself, I don't want to work under this negative influence. I'm here to rest and restore my soul, not to have yet another battle to prove to somebody that I can achieve something with one arm. And I had a great burden lifted from my shoulders as I said to myself, I don't want to take this course.

I went back and talked to the teacher, and asked for a refund of my money from the administration, which they gratefully gave me. That night, I exploded with disappointment and anger, but after an AA meeting, a wonderful woman approached me and said, "Why don't you go over to the Wooden Boat School? You could learn how to make a boat." I said, "Good heavens, if I can't make a basket, I can hardly make a boat." She insisted, "No, go over and meet the head of the school."

So I went over and introduced myself to a Rich Helsinger, who turned out to be a fellow Philadelphian. He told me that a friend of his from Baltimore wanted to learn to build a nutshell pram designed by Joel White. He said that this friend could be my partner—together we could build this boat, and that he would be there to help me, which was what Wooden Boat School was about. And, in fact, that was what I was able to do. I signed up, nervously went over for my first day of class, and eventually was able to build a sailboat, finish it, paint it, and rig it. I then went back to Wooden Boat School to learn how to sail it. And in that wonderful, single act of generosity and educational openness, my soul was restored.

Here then, in the spirit of the Maine coast, are three classic New England chowder recipes. I think of my Maine boat-building experiences every time I cook these meals.

Clam Chowder

2 dozen large hard-shell clams, well scrubbed, or 3 (7-ounce) cans
   minced clams
1 (10¾-ounce) can chicken broth
4 slices bacon, diced
½ cup chopped celery
1 large onion, chopped
1 small green bell pepper, seeded and chopped
2 large carrots, scraped and thinly sliced
4 large potatoes, peeled and chopped into ¾-inch dice
2 medium white turnips, scraped and diced
1 (12-ounce) can evaporated milk
Salt and pepper to taste

FOR *FRESH CLAMS:* Steam them open, strain and reserve the
liquid, and chop the clams coarsely.

For *canned clams:* strain and reserve the liquid. Reserve the
clams.

To the clam liquid, add chicken broth to equal 4 cups. Reserve
the liquid.

In a soup kettle, render the bacon. Remove and reserve the
diced bacon. In the fat, cook the celery, onion, and bell pepper until
the onion is golden brown. Add the carrots, potatoes, and turnips,
stirring to coat them well. Combine with the diced bacon, the clams,
the reserved clam liquid, and the evaporated milk, and cook on very
low heat for half an hour, or until the potato is tender.

SERVES: 6

Crab Chowder

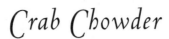

1 medium potato, peeled and diced

1 cup water

2 teaspoons butter

1 small onion, peeled and grated

½ teaspoon paprika

1 teaspoon salt

¼ teaspoon white pepper

3 cups milk

1 cup light cream

2 tablespoons quick-cooking tapioca

1½ cups flaked crabmeat or 2 (6-ounce) cans crabmeat

3 tablespoons cognac or dry sherry or Madeira

Finely chopped parsley, for garnish

IN A SAUCEPAN, combine the potato and water. Bring the water to a boil and cook the potato, covered, for 20 minutes, or until it is tender. Reserve the potato and the cooking liquid.

In a large saucepan, heat the butter and cook the onion for 3 minutes. Stir in the paprika, salt, and pepper. Add the milk, cream, and tapioca. Bring the mixture rapidly to a boil, stirring constantly; reduce the heat and simmer the mixture, uncovered, stirring occasionally, until the tapioca is dissolved and the liquid is smooth. Stir in the crabmeat, potato, and potato cooking liquid. Continue to simmer the soup for 10 minutes. At serving time, stir in the wine of your choice. Garnish the chowder with chopped parsley.

SERVES: 6

Corn Chowder

6 slices bacon, diced

3 medium onions, chopped

3 large potatoes, peeled and diced

2 cups water

1 teaspoon salt

¼ teaspoon pepper

1 (20-ounce) can cream-style corn

4 cups milk

IN A LARGE SAUCEPAN, render the bacon; drain it on absorbent paper and reserve. In the bacon fat, cook the onions until translucent. Add the diced potatoes, stirring to coat them well. Add the water and salt and pepper. Bring the liquid to a boil, reduce the heat, and simmer the potato, covered, for 20 minutes, or until it is tender. Stir in the corn and milk. Heat the chowder thoroughly. Serve it garnished with the diced bacon.

SERVES: 6 TO 8

A MONSIGNOR CAME to my father to have his teeth fixed, and while he was in the dentist's chair, he complained to my father about hurting him.

My father said, "Monsignor, offer it up!"

The monsignor replied, "Dr. Curry, go to hell!"

Carrot Puree

4 cups sliced carrots (about 1 ½ pounds)
1 celery stalk, chopped
2 cups chopped leeks (white and some green)
½-inch piece bay leaf
6 sprigs of parsley
6 cups chicken stock
1 cup half-and-half
3 tablespoons butter
⅛ teaspoon freshly grated nutmeg
¼ teaspoon white pepper
½ teaspoon freshly grated lemon peel
½ teaspoon brown sugar
½ cup coarsely grated carrot
¼ cup heavy cream
Salt to taste
Croutons or toast rounds
Minced fresh parsley or mint, for garnish

COOK THE SLICED CARROTS, celery, leeks, bay leaf, and parsley in 1 cup of the stock, covered, until very soft. Remove the bay leaf and puree the mixture, adding more stock as needed. Force this through a fine sieve; add the remaining stock, half-and-half, butter, nutmeg, pepper, and lemon peel. Heat, but do not boil. Melt the brown sugar in a saucepan and cook, stirring, for 3 to 4 minutes. Add the grated carrot and heavy cream, cover, and cook for 5 minutes, or until the carrot is tender-crisp. Add this to the hot soup, adjusting seasonings and adding salt as needed. Add croutons and sprinkle with parsley for garnish.

SERVES: 4 TO 6

Easter

*L*ord Jesus Christ, you have opened up to us the fullness of life by your death and resurrection. As your sisters and brothers, redeemed by your blood, we come to you in gratitude and exaltation. Help us celebrate this gift by giving us the desire to talk to another about our hope in your resurrection. We humbly ask this of you, who live and reign with the Father and the Holy Spirit, one God, for ever and ever. Amen.

RICK CURRY, S.J.

D EER I SLE, M AINE, holds a special place in my heart because it was there, during a four-month sabbatical in 1988, that I attended the Wooden Boat School and learned to build a small sailboat. That whole sabbatical in Maine was both life giving and life renewing. The uniqueness of the island community was evident even in the way its members worshipped. The picturesque Roman Catholic parish of Our Lady, Star of the Sea, served its own parishioners at 9:00 A.M. and welcomed the Episcopal community under the patronage of St. Brendan, the Navigator, at 11:00 A.M. The only liturgical accoutrements that needed changing were the candlesticks, and that not for reasons of orthodoxy but rather because one of the congregations included a world-class potter who had donated the candlesticks to his community whereas the other group of worshippers stuck with a more traditional brass set.

On one Sunday morning in August both parishes were abuzz because the bishop of the Episcopalian diocese of Maine was coming to Deer Isle to address both congregations. Bishop Edward Chalfant, decked out in gorgeous red robes with elaborate lace trim, appeared larger than life in the sanctuary of this simple country church. He looked every inch a church dignitary. He greeted both congregations warmly and thanked the Roman Catholic parishioners for being so generous in sharing their space with their Protestant neighbors. He reminded both groups that not only did they share their everyday lives with one another but they also shared a faith in the most fundamental belief of Christianity, the resurrection of our Lord Jesus Christ.

He then read from the Holy Gospel according to John 20:1–9. This is the account of Mary Magdalen's discovery in the early morning that Jesus' tomb was empty. Her message produced a flurry of activity and a lot of running back and forth as apostles hurried to the tomb and tried to figure out what happened. John seemed to be the only disciple who got it. The others, as the Scripture says, "did not yet understand the Scripture that he had to rise from the dead." Then the good bishop of Maine developed in a masterly way the lesson that faith is fragile and has to be nurtured if it is to grow. "Do not be discouraged if your faith is fragile," the bishop exclaimed, "but strengthen this gift by talking about your hope in the resurrection with one another." Then with a twinkle in his eye, he said, "Even talk to Catholics about it."

As is the custom of both these congregations after a special occasion there was a potluck meal awaiting us outside on the lawn overlooking the majestic harbor. This lunch included wonderful soups, stews, salads, and pies—and a greater meaning for me of Easter.

THERE COMES THAT VERY AWKWARD TIME in a young boy's life when he announces to his parents that he's leaving for the religious life, or at least asks their blessing for permission to leave for the religious life. It came to be that time for me after graduation from high school, when I announced to my parents that I wanted to join the Jesuits. My father had taken my sister's departure to the convent very hard. I think she paved the way and made it much easier for me. My father saw that my sister was very happy, and thought that if I could have just half the amount of happiness that my sister seemed to have, then I would be fine. But my father, ever a practical man, wanted to know if, in fact, my chances of being accepted were strong or not, because he certainly wanted me to cover myself by applying to college. That was the end of the discussion.

After dinner, my mother asked, "Now, are you really serious about joining the Jesuits? Do you really want to be accepted?" I assured her that I did. She said, "Okay, then ask your father for the car. We're going for a ride." My mother instructed me to go to Twenty-second and Green Street in downtown Philadelphia, near the art museum.

Twenty-second and Green Street houses a convent known as the Convent of Divine Love, which houses a contemplative group of nuns affectionately known as the Pink Sisters, who are, in fact, officially known as the Sisters of the Holy Spirit of Perpetual Adoration. They are known as the Pink Sisters because their habit is a *gaudete/laetare* pink. The Convent of Divine Love had always been a favorite devotional spot of my mother's, and during times of crisis, my mother would call on the sisters for help with divine intervention. It's a cloistered order of nuns, and when we rang the bell, a little wheel turned and we heard a small voice that said, *"Laudate Jesus Christus"* ("Praise be to Jesus Christ"). My mother answered, "Forever and ever." The sister inquired, "Yes, how can I help you?" My mother said, "I would like you to pray for my son's acceptance into the Society of Jesus." The sister said, "Absolutely, no problem, count on his acceptance." My mother asked, "Now, Sister, is there something I can get you, or could you use some money?" The sister said, "We need soap." My mother said, "Oxydol?" meaning detergent for washing clothes. "No," the sister replied, "body soap." My mother informed her that she would take care of it.

The next day my mother called John Wanamaker's, and a case of lavender soap was sent to the sisters. When my mother was near death, she told me she had been sending lavender soap to the sisters for quite some time, and she hoped that I would continue to take care of them afterward.

Potage aux Fines Herbes

1 cup chopped sorrel
½ cup chopped lettuce
½ cup chopped chervil
½ cup chopped watercress
¾ cup chopped leeks (white only)
2 cloves garlic, minced
2 teaspoons minced fresh dill
1 tablespoon butter
½ tablespoon unbleached flour
2 cups brown chicken stock
1 teaspoon minced fresh savory
½ teaspoon minced fresh basil
1 cup peeled and diced potato
1½ cups half-and-half or milk
2 egg yolks, beaten
½ cup heavy cream
Salt to taste
White pepper to taste
Watercress sprigs, for garnish

SAUTÉ THE SORREL, lettuce, chervil, watercress, leeks, garlic, and dill in the butter for 5 minutes, making sure that they are well coated. Sprinkle the flour over and cook, stirring, for 3 minutes, gradually adding the stock. Cook and stir until smooth. Add the savory, basil, and potato.

Cover, bring to a boil, and cook until the potato is soft. Puree the mixture and reheat with added half-and-half. Beat together the yolks and the heavy cream, whisk with ½ cup of the hot soup, and return this to the rest of the soup. Reheat, but do not boil. Adjust the taste with salt and pepper. Garnish with watercress. SERVES: 4

WHY DO WE SO FEAR being different? I guess the reality is that we will be ostracized. Or at least we *fear* that we will be ostracized. And yet, as Christians, Jesus asks us to be different, to stand alone. Jesus Himself was different. He always went against the mainstream. I love to quote St. Francis de Sales when he says, "I will praise the Creator with the face he gave me." It's only in our total acceptance of ourselves as we are, in giving that back to the Father through Jesus, that we can truly celebrate the personhood He has given us. And so I think that the disabled are reminders of life's fragility, but also celebrations of difference and individuality. It is only by appreciating our own peculiarities and the peculiarities of others that we can celebrate what it means to be part of the human family.

We're all part of communities, whether it's a small religious community, whether it's our church, whether it's our neighborhood, or our workplace. Sometimes we belong to many communities. The asceticism that one needs to follow the lure is often found in the difficulties that we find in our communities. There's enough asceticism living in a family, or living in a community, that one doesn't need much more. We certainly would like everyone to act in a certain way. We want them to act the way we act. We want our actions to be totally acceptable. But, in fact, Jesus says no. He stands alone and says that the one yardstick by which we should judge ourselves is Himself, and that we should get excited about others judging themselves that way, too. It's only in our acceptance of ourselves as we are that we can praise the Creator with the face He gave us.

Asparagus Soup

1 pound asparagus, tough ends removed
2 cups loosely packed chopped red-leaf, escarole, or any soft-leaf
   lettuce
4 green onions, chopped (white and some green)
1 clove garlic, minced
1 tablespoon minced fresh tarragon
2 tablespoons butter and/or rendered chicken fat
3 tablespoons rice flour
5 cups brown chicken stock
½ cup heavy cream
2 teaspoons fresh lemon juice
½ teaspoon salt
¼ teaspoon black pepper
Minced fresh parsley and/or chives, for garnish
Paprika, for garnish

CUT THE TIPS FROM THE ASPARAGUS and set aside. Cut the remaining stalks into 1-inch pieces and sauté with the lettuce, onions, garlic, and tarragon in the butter until they are soft and lightly browned. Sprinkle with the flour and continue to cook, stirring, for 2 minutes.

Stir in the stock and the asparagus tips and cook until slightly thickened, or until the asparagus is very soft. Puree and reheat with cream, but do not boil. Add the lemon juice and adjust seasoning with salt and pepper. Garnish with parsley and paprika.

SERVES: 4 TO 6

ONE OF THE PERKS OF LIVING in New York City is that there is such a variety of people that you would not normally encounter in a more homogeneous community. One of the more exotic persons that I've had the privilege to meet was Herbert Mayer. Herbert was the husband of Ann Gardner, who was our original director of music for the National Theatre Workshop of the Handicapped. He was a brilliant musician and was robbed of a great concert-maestro career by Adolf Hitler. Herbert escaped Nazi Germany and found work as a conductor in New York, Hollywood, and Boston, before eventually settling into married life in New York City and a career in training opera singers. We became fast friends, and he loved to spend hours asking me about Jesuit life. He had enormous respect for the Jesuits, but was puzzled by our celibacy. This resulted in many lively conversations, from which I always left the beneficiary.

Final vows come to a Jesuit many years after his first vows, but they represent the final approbation of the Society of Jesus for its members. First vows are a private affair, whereas final vows are intended as a public celebration. There is an exquisitely beautiful church in New York City run by the Dominicans, known as St. Vincent Ferrer, on East Sixty-sixth Street. It is one of the most beautiful Roman Catholic churches in the city. Because I had been teaching at the Dominican Academy, I was familiar with the Dominicans and, when it came time for my final vows, I was invited to hold them in their church. I was attracted to the church not only because of its beauty, but also

EASTER

171

because it is totally accessible to persons with disabilities. I knew that my students at the National Theatre Workshop of the Handicapped would be able to attend, and I wanted them to participate in the liturgy. Of course, I invited Ann Gardner and her husband, Herbert, to come. Herbert Mayer would never be associated with churchgoing, but Ann convinced him to attend, assuring him that the service would include some extraordinary music. However, she warned him ahead of time that he would have to behave himself in the church. Almost immediately upon entering St. Vincent Ferrer's, Herbert started to fuss, and Ann admonished him, saying, "Herbert, behave!" He kept it up nonetheless. Finally, once they had reached their pew, he turned to her and said, "I have something to tell you. I have been here before." "What do you mean, you've been here before?" Ann asked. "This is where I was married to my first wife," Herbert replied, referring to a marriage that had lasted less than a year. "I hope that Rick's vows last longer than that marriage," Herbert continued. As I walked up the aisle at the procession, I was delighted to see Ann and Herbert in attendance, but was surprised to find Ann smiling ear to ear, as though she had been giggling.

Potage Saint-Cloud

6 cups shelled green peas

6 cups chicken stock

Bouquet garni of:

    ½ onion

    1 clove garlic

    1 sprig of thyme

    1 sprig of chervil

    4 sprigs of parsley

    3 basil leaves

    2 green onions, with tops, cut up

    1 bay leaf

1 teaspoon turmeric

1 cup heavy cream

½ teaspoon salt

⅛ teaspoon white pepper

Dry sherry to taste

Minced fresh chervil or parsley, for garnish

Croutons, for garnish

COMBINE THE PEAS, stock, bouquet garni, and turmeric; cover and bring to a boil. Cook for 5 minutes, until the peas are tender-crisp. Remove ½ cup of the peas and reserve. Continue cooking the remaining mixture for 30 minutes. Discard the bouquet garni. Puree, and then reheat with cream and season with salt and pepper. Add the reserved peas and the sherry. Garnish with chervil and croutons.

SERVES: 6

WHEN I WAS WRITING *The Secrets of Jesuit Breadmaking,* I was working in anonymity, and no one was sending me any recipes. When the word got out that I would be writing a soup book after the bread book, I received some wonderful letters from Jesuits all over the world. A very good friend of mine, a New York Province Jesuit named Jerry Blaszczak, who was for a time the novice master of the New York–Maryland Province and had taught theology in Africa, sent me this wonderful letter about Holy Week.

Dear Rick:

Holy Week in Mexico is the time for "Missions." Many young and not so young Mexican Catholics give up holidays to spend la semana santa *in rural outposts,* ranchos, *where people are lucky if they see a priest two or three times a year. The "missionaries," sent by their own local communities, run religious reflections for adults and teenagers, and offer religious instruction for children. They visit the aged and homebound, and conduct Holy Week services as best they can.*

The rural zones of Mexico are a land of shattered dreams. The weary, overworked earth cannot feed her children. It is not rich enough; it is often in the hands of landlords who live in distant cities and who have little care for the land or those who till it. Most able-bodied men have no choice but to leave the ones they love and head for El Norte.

After celebrating the Easter vigil, the misa de la gloria, *Mexican* campesinos, *visiting missionaries, and, on occasion, stray gringo padres gather for a* convivencia, *a communal*

feast, in which, in central and northern Mexico, a rich soup
is served.

I myself have been fortunate enough to travel to Mexico, and to visit my friend Laura Esquivel, the author of *Like Water for Chocolate.* Here is her wonderful soup: perfect for Lent and Holy Week.

Mexican Soup

3 carrots, peeled and sliced

2 turnips, peeled and quartered

1 celery stalk, chopped

1 bunch scallions, cleaned and cut into 1-inch pieces

1 onion, stuck with 3 cloves

10 cups water

Pepper and salt to taste

1 green bell pepper

2 tomatoes, peeled and diced

3 tablespoons olive oil

4 medium onions, minced

2 cloves garlic, minced

1 pound ground beef

2 eggs, lightly beaten

½ cup bread crumbs

1 teaspoon powdered saffron

1 teaspoon chili powder

1 cup chopped parsley

1 teaspoon dried mint leaves or ¼ cup fresh leaves

IN A KETTLE, put the carrots, turnips, celery, scallions, and the onion stuck with cloves. Add the water, pepper, and salt. Bring to a boil, then reduce the heat to low, cover and cook for 1 hour.

Meanwhile, peel the green bell pepper as follows: Place your pepper directly over one of your gas burners until the skin cracks. Before this happens, it will actually burn—that is, turn black in certain places—but don't let this concern you; the charring will impart a smoky flavor. To peel, place the pepper under running water and scrape off the charred portions with a knife. Remove the white seeds and dice the pepper.

To peel the tomatoes, impale them on a fork and immerse them for a few seconds in boiling water, which will "pop" the skin and make them easy to peel. (Note: If you have an electric stove, rather than gas, use the same method to peel your green peppers. You'll get the desired result, but without the smoky flavor.)

In a skillet, heat the oil and sauté the onion until golden brown. In a bowl, mix the contents of the skillet with the tomatoes, green bell pepper, garlic, beef, eggs, bread crumbs, saffron, chili powder, and half the parsley and the mint leaves. Form small balls, about the size of marbles.

When the vegetable broth is done, drop the meatballs in the gently boiling broth. Let them rise to the surface and continue to cook for another 5 to 8 minutes (no longer, for it would tend to soften or disintegrate the meatballs). Discard the cloves. Add the rest of the parsley and serve.

SERVES: 6 TO 8

No cookbook can be complete without acknowledging the marvelous cuisine that comes from the state of California. The year was 1849, and the Jesuits were being terribly persecuted in the Turin province of Italy, forcing most of them to flee. They were very taken with the work of Father De Smet, the Belgian who was opening up the West, so the Rocky Mountains became a real mission, and fired the imaginations of the Italian Jesuits. Two Jesuit fathers, Father Nobili and Father Accolti, were in Portland, Oregon, and heard the news that there were many Irish coming into San Francisco in 1849 for the Gold Rush. They wrote to Rome, asking for permission to go down into California to start the California Mission, which would become the California Province, to minister to all these Catholics. Father Nobili and Father Accolti anticipated permission by going down to work among the people. Father Nobili went farther and founded Santa Clara Mission, where the Jesuits began a grammar school and eventually a college, which is a very famous university today. Sadly, he suffered a tragic injury: when building the mission, a nail went into his foot, which eventually led to his death. He died of tetanus while in his thirties.

Two years later, the letter arrived from Rome telling the Jesuits, "No, do not go into California, remain in Oregon," but, of course, they were already there, so it has always been a little joke that the California Province was founded on disobedience. In 1851, the Jesuits founded Santa Clara University.

California has always been a wondrous state for me, although sometimes I am bewildered by Californians themselves. I often make trips to California, particularly to the Los Angeles area, in hopes of interesting the film industry in supporting the work that I'm doing in theater education for the disabled. On one visit to California, I went into a small shop, and there was a very attractive little kitchen clock that I thought would make a wonderful gift for a friend of mine, but was afraid that it would be too expensive. Upon examining the clock, I discovered that it was a plastic reproduction, and actually quite nice, but that it was only fourteen dollars, so I was suspicious that it might be more of a toy than an actual clock. I carried it over to the clerk behind the counter, and said to him, "I hope this clock works." He looked at me and said, "With your decor?"

Of course, the soups and the foods of California are legendary.

Avocado Soup

3 large soft-ripe avocados
4 green onions, thinly sliced (use part of tops)
1 (14½-ounce) can chicken broth
2 tablespoons lime or lemon juice
½ teaspoon salt
½ teaspoon ground cumin
Pinch of cayenne pepper
2 tablespoons tequila
2 cups half-and-half
Thin lime slices, for garnish

PEEL AND PIT THE AVOCADOS; dice them coarsely (you should have about 4 cups). Place in a blender or food processor with the green onions, broth, lime juice, salt, cumin, and cayenne pepper. Process until very smooth.

Pour into a large glass bowl and blend in the tequila, then the half-and-half. Cover and refrigerate until thoroughly chilled (2 to 3 hours). Stir well; garnish with a lime slice.

SERVES: 6

IN 1982, MY ASSISTANT at the National Theatre Workshop of the Handicapped, Louis LoRe, received a call from a gentleman asking if we had an actress available who would fit the rigorous description of being a midget, hunchbacked, and blind. Immediately, Louis thought that this call was a prank, but ever polite, he dutifully informed the gentleman, "We do have some little people, some blind students, and a woman who has suffered a spinal injury." The caller said that he was producing a movie about the fourteenth-century Dominican Margaret of Costello, and that he wanted an authentically disabled actress to play the role. Louis encouraged him to make a trip to the school to see our talent. He arrived, and shortly thereafter was impressed by the poise and the beauty of a blind actress named Lucia Puccia. He quickly negotiated to have her fly to Italy, to film *The Life of Little Margaret* on location in the twelfth-century walled city of Costello. He admitted that he had no idea how he would handle directing a blind actress who had a guide dog, and so he offered me a part in order to enlist my services. He said that the role he had in mind for me was of a one-armed prisoner who refuses to accept God's will. One month later, we flew to Rome, where we were met by the director and brought to Citta de Costello in the Umbrian Hills. This medieval villa was magical. There, in the church in the center of Costello, under glass and beneath the altar, were the miraculously preserved remains of Margaret, clothed in her habit. Every morning after Mass I would visit this relic and ask for a blessing on the day.

We were living in a house run by the most hospitable nuns. Every day was an adventure. For one scene, we required rain, and the local volunteer fire department had been enlisted to provide it by means of their decrepit horse-drawn water tanks. Making a film implies delays, so by the time we needed their services, the firemen were drunk. Not only that, but once filming had started, they wanted to be featured in each scene, and made every effort to ensure that this would happen. Needless to say, those scenes eventually found their way to the cutting room floor. The sisters with whom we stayed worked assiduously on our behalf, and at the end of a particularly long day, we returned home for a supper of bread, prosciutto, cheese, and eggplant soup.

Eggplant Soup

4 tablespoons olive oil

1 clove garlic, peeled and finely chopped

2 medium onions, peeled and chopped

3 tablespoons flour

1 large eggplant, peeled and chopped (about 2 pounds)

4 cups homemade chicken or veal stock or 3 (10½-ounce) cans
*   chicken or beef broth*

⅓ cup chopped parsley

½ teaspoon oregano

Salt and pepper to taste

Grated Parmesan cheese to taste

HEAT THE OIL in a large saucepan and cook the garlic and onions until translucent. Stir in the flour and cook the mixture over gentle heat for a few minutes. Add the eggplant, stock, parsley, and oregano.

Bring to a boil, reduce the heat, and simmer, covered, for 30 minutes. (You may also allow the soup to cool, then puree it in a food processor. Bring it to a temperature for serving.) Season to taste with pepper, salt, and Parmesan cheese.

SERVES: 6

Two things I believe that everyone needs are a spiritual adviser and a historian. A spiritual adviser will lead you sensibly to a relation with almighty God, and a historian will keep you humble, because you will realize that no matter what problems you are having, you're not the first person to be having them, nor did you invent the problem.

Cream of Carrot Soup

6 large carrots, scraped and grated
1 small onion, peeled and chopped
1 ½ teaspoons sugar
½ teaspoon salt
1 ½ cups water
3 tablespoons butter
3 tablespoons flour
½ teaspoon salt
¼ teaspoon white pepper
3 cups milk
1 cup heavy cream
Finely chopped parsley, for garnish

COMBINE THE CARROTS, onion, sugar, salt, and water in a large saucepan. Bring to a boil, reduce the heat, and simmer, covered, for 20 minutes. Puree the mixture in a food processor. Reserve.

Heat the butter in the top of a large double boiler, add the flour, and cook over gentle heat for a few minutes. Stir in the salt and pepper. Gradually add the milk, stirring constantly, until the mixture is thickened and smooth. Stir in the carrot puree. Over simmering water, cook the soup, covered, for 20 minutes. Stir in the cream and bring the soup to serving temperature. Garnish with chopped parsley.

SERVES: 6

WHEN I WAS A NOVICE, and we would celebrate other Jesuits' Golden Jubilees, I always thought of these devoted members as being confined to wheelchairs and feeble. Now that I have completed more than forty years of service, these career Jesuits are looking younger and much more vigorous. I am always edified by what they say after fifty years of service. With the advent of the Internet, their wisdom can be easily disseminated, and the Jesuits have an Internet service courtesy of *Company* magazine. The August 24 newsletter features a snippet from the reflections of Father Michael Campbell-Johnston, a British Jesuit who had at one time been the provincial of the British Province, and who is now the director of Jesuit Development in El Salvador. I was deeply moved by his remarks, and in particular by one sentence, in which he wrote, "Ultimately, all that really matters is where, in our own devotions, we have been able to increase by even a little the amount of love that exists in the world."

Cream of Chicken and Apple Soup

3 tablespoons butter

2 medium tart apples, peeled, cored, and chopped

1 medium onion, chopped

2 tablespoons flour

½ teaspoon salt

3 cups homemade chicken stock or 2 (10½-ounce) cans chicken
    broth plus water to equal 3 cups

¾ cup dry white wine

1½ cups light cream

1 cup diced cooked chicken

Salt to taste

White pepper to taste

HEAT THE BUTTER in a large saucepan and cook the apple and onion until the onion is translucent. Add the flour and salt, stirring the mixture. Add the stock and the wine.

Bring to a boil, reduce the heat, and simmer, stirring, for 10 minutes. Allow to cool slightly.

Whirl the mixture 2 cupfuls at a time in a food processor, until it is smooth. Return to the saucepan along with cream and chicken. Bring to a serving temperature. Season to taste with salt and pepper.

SERVES: 4 TO 6

WHILE IN AMSTERDAM, I went to see the Church of St. Francis Xavier, about two blocks away from the Anne Frank house. I was really delighted by the beauty of this church and went early on Saturday to see what time the Mass schedule was, because it was there that I wanted to participate in Mass the following day.

When I arrived at the church, I noticed an absolutely breathtaking wooden statue of St. Alphonsus Rodriguez, the patron of Jesuit brothers. It depicted St. Alphonsus leaping from his chair, with one hand holding the chair and the other clutching rosary beads, and on the bottom of the chair was written, *"Va voy, Señor"* ("I'm coming, Lord"). It was the tradition of St. Alphonsus that every time there was a knock on the door, he would say, "I'm coming, Lord," as if he were responding to Jesus' coming to the door. It was how he treated every visitor who came to his *colegio* at Salamanca.

When I arrived the following morning, I was disappointed to find that the Mass schedule had been changed, and I would have to wait for about forty minutes for the next Mass. I entered the back of the church and discovered a priest in full cassock standing in the back. I said hello, and he greeted me warmly. I introduced myself to him as a Jesuit, and he was delighted.

In the course of the conversation I remarked to him how happy I was to see the statue of St. Alphonsus Rodriguez, a rare event. He struck me as somewhat dismayed by this remark. I explained to him that I was a Jesuit brother. He showed further dismay, and it was as if a steel trapdoor had dropped down, as though he really no longer believed me. He then began to ask probing questions. He inquired as to which province I was from; I told him I was from the Maryland Province, although I was working in the New York Province, and living in New York City. I told him that I ran a theater school for the disabled. I further informed him that I was in the process of writing a book and was interviewing Jesuit brothers throughout the world, but had been delayed in a visit to Cologne and thought that the delay afforded a wonderful opportunity to visit Amsterdam.

I then asked if I could use the bathroom in the community. He showed his reluctance, and finally admitted to me his suspicion that I wasn't a Jesuit. I asked him why. He told me that it was because I did what he believed Jesuit brothers didn't do; namely, Jesuit brothers rarely traveled.

Then he asked me about a fellow Jesuit in my province, with whom I was familiar, and he told me that he thought he was related to him, and was compiling a family history. I told him that when I returned to my province, I would have this Jesuit write on his behalf. He said to me, still very much doubting my sincerity, "Well, if you are a Jesuit, let me accompany you into the community," so I was able to use the bathroom, which was a great relief to me.

The Mass followed shortly thereafter, and I was able to participate in, actually, a beautiful service. But you can imagine my delight when a year later I was able to send him a copy of my book to prove that I was, in fact, a Jesuit brother and no great impostor.

Orange and Tomato Soup

2 tablespoons butter or margarine

1 small onion, finely chopped

1 small clove garlic, minced or pressed

¼ teaspoon ground cumin

⅛ teaspoon white pepper

1 large (28-ounce) can tomatoes

Grated rind and juice of 1 large orange

1¾ cups rich homemade chicken broth or 1 (14½-ounce) can
    chicken broth

Salt to taste

Sour cream and additional grated orange rind, for garnish

In a 3- to 4-quart saucepan over medium heat, melt the butter. Add the onion and cook until soft but not browned. Mix in the garlic, cumin, and pepper. Then add the tomatoes (break up with a fork) and their liquid. Mix in the orange rind and juice and chicken broth.

Bring to a boil, cover, reduce heat, and simmer for 30 minutes.

In a blender or food processor, process the soup, about half at a time, until smooth. Return the puree to the cooking pan; taste, and add salt if needed.

Reheat to serving temperature. Serve hot, garnishing each serving with a dollop of sour cream and a sprinkling of orange rind.

SERVES: 6

THERE WERE ALSO SUBTLE LESSONS in the novitiate. Our superior would tell us, "Never shelter a superior from bad news. For instance, when you're in the refectory and you're putting out dishes on the table and they're chipped, don't hide them. Don't give the best to the superior, give the chipped ones to the superior, so he'll see that the community needs new dishes." Well, the poor superior, every chipped dish, every chipped cup, was always set at his place.

Lobster Bisque

Lobster shells, remaining from 6 or more servings

2 cloves garlic, coarsely chopped

2 medium onions, coarsely chopped

2 bay leaves

4 peppercorns, crushed

½ teaspoon dried thyme

1 teaspoon sugar

4 cups water

4 chicken bouillon cubes

3 tablespoons butter

3 tablespoons flour

2 cups light cream, scalded

Salt to taste

Canned crab or lobster or shrimp, optional

Dry sherry, optional

COMBINE THE SEAFOOD, including the lobster shells, garlic, onions, bay leaves, peppercorns, thyme, sugar, water, and bouillon in a soup kettle. Bring to a boil, reduce the heat, and simmer, covered, for 45 minutes. Strain the broth through a fine sieve, making sure that all shells are emptied of liquid and the meaty parts are squeezed dry. Reserve the broth.

Heat the butter in a saucepan and cook the flour in it for a few minutes. Gradually add the cream, stirring, until the mixture is thickened and smooth. Stir in reserved broth. Correct the seasoning with salt to taste.

If desired, add crab, lobster, or shrimp (pick over crab and lobster to remove any tendons and, if you intend to freeze the soup, do not add the solids until after the bisque has come fully to room temperature). The addition of sherry, to taste, is a pleasant embellishment.

SERVES: 4 TO 6

WHEN YOU ARE BORN DISABLED, particularly with an overt sign of disability like I have (I am missing a right forearm), you spend an awful lot of time answering questions about what happened to you. If I had a nickel for every time I have been compelled to insist "I was born this way," I would have an endowed theater. When I started to work with other disabled students at the National Theatre Workshop of the Handicapped, I began to hear them tell similar stories of people asking them about their arms, about their legs, about their wheelchairs, about their disabilities. One night in theater class, we decided to analyze what was really going on when people asked us how we became disabled, or what happened to us. We found that there were some striking similarities in our situations. One was that they usually asked us in a public place or in the open air. Two, we realized that they were not asking about us but about what *happened* to us. The third thing we discovered, which is also very curious, is that if we gave them an answer that they weren't particularly ready to hear, the response was one of disappointment or even of anger. We began to draw a couple of conclusions from these similarities. One was that by asking us in a public area, they seemed to be treating us as public property. Two, they weren't really, genuinely, interested in *us* but in seeing how they could avoid becoming disabled themselves. And, three, everyone seemed to have an opinion about disability from the able-bodied point of view and did not seem to be willing to consider the disabled point of view. Fortunately, most of the students who shared with us were very secure with their disability, and found great humor in some of the incidents.

Once, in New York City, I was standing at a red light at Fifty-sixth Street and Sixth Avenue when a woman came up to me and said, in a loud voice, in front of other people, "Hey, what happened to your arm?" I told her that nothing happened to my arm, and was going to add, "Because I was born this way," but before I had the opportunity, she interjected, "Look, I was in Vietnam, and just because you lost your arm in Vietnam doesn't mean that you don't have to tell me," and with that she started to curse at a loud volume, which was embarrassing not only to me, but also to everybody else around. Her assumption was that I had lost my arm in Vietnam and was afraid to tell her—somehow she found this offensive.

One of my students, who happens to be blind, was standing on a street corner, and a man came up to him, took him by the arm, and said, "I'll take you there." My student said, "Take me where?" The presumption is that if a blind person is in a five-mile radius of the Lighthouse, which is an institution for the blind, then the blind person must be going there. Another blind student had a man come up to him and ask, stuttering, "H-h-h-how did you go blind?" And my student, who is very funny, said, "I went blind shortly after I stopped stuttering." At which point, he explained to me that the man stopped stuttering, because his expletives were in the clearest language he could imagine.

But the children are the most refreshing, and the most honest. And because I think adults are getting a little more comfortable with disability, they don't seem to tell their children to be afraid of us, or admonish them when they ask us why we are different. I had a candid example of this just recently. In our school in Belfast, Maine, we offered a summer theater workshop for the able-bodied children of the town, which was taught by our disabled faculty. A little six-year-old boy came up and said to me, "What happened to your arm?" I replied, "I was born this way." And the little boy said, "Cool!" It was the most delightful response, I think, that I've ever received.

Brazilian Black Bean Soup

2 cups dried black beans
10 cups water
2 (4-ounce) packages dried beef, chopped
¼ pound slab bacon, cubed
1 unsalted pig's foot
½ pound smoked pork
½ pound Spanish garlic sausage, cut in rounds
½ pound smoked tongue

COMBINE THE BEANS AND WATER in a soup kettle. Bring to a boil and cook for 10 minutes over high heat.

Remove from the heat and allow to stand, covered, for 1 hour. Add the dried beef, bacon, pig's foot, smoked pork, garlic sausage, and tongue to the kettle. Return to a boil, reduce the heat, and simmer the beans, covered, for 2½ hours, or until the beans are very tender. Remove the pig's foot, smoked pork, and tongue. Dice the meat and return it to the kettle, discarding any fat and bone.

SERVES: 4 TO 6

WHEN I WAS LIVING IN AMERICA HOUSE, where the Jesuit weekly magazine is published, the minister of our community, Vincent Carney, passed away. America House is located in Midtown Manhattan, right behind Carnegie Hall and next door to the New York Health and Racquet Club. When Vinnie died, we sent his body from the hospital to the undertaker to be embalmed, and then we all gathered upstairs in the recreation room right before dinner to wait for the telephone call from the undertaker. He was going to call when he arrived so we could go downstairs to greet Vinnie's body and carry the casket into the second-floor LaFarge Lounge, where Father Carney would be waked. Around 5:50 the telephone range and Father Joseph O'Hare, the superior of our community and now the president of Fordham University, answered the phone and said to the Jesuits gathered there, "Vinnie's arrived, let's go down and get him."

When we got downstairs, we discovered that the hearse was not directly in front of the building but, because of the traffic, to the left, and directly in front of the New York Health and Racquet Club. We had all gathered solemnly to bring Vinnie's body out of the hearse, when we turned and saw two young women in leotards coming out of the Health and Racquet Club fixing their hair and lighting up cigarettes. One of the women froze suddenly and, with eyes the size of coffee saucers, looked at the casket, looked at us, looked back at her girlfriend, and said, "Oh, my God, no more cigarette smoking for me, I'm going back and doing more exercise."

Mussel Soup Billy-Bi

2 quarts uncooked mussels in shells (about 3 pounds)
2 tablespoons butter
¼ teaspoon paprika
4 shallots, finely chopped
3 sprigs of parsley
¼ teaspoon whole white peppercorns
1 cup dry white wine
1½ to 2 cups fish broth or 1 (14½-ounce) can chicken broth
2 cups heavy cream
Salt to taste
Chopped Italian flat-leaf parsley, for garnish

DISCARD ANY MUSSELS that have opened. Scrape off barnacles and scrub mussels with a stiff brush under running water; drain.

In a 4- to 5-quart kettle over medium heat, melt the butter. Add the paprika and shallots and cook, stirring, until soft but not browned. Add the mussels in shells, parsley, peppercorns, and wine. Bring to a boil, cover, reduce heat, and simmer until mussels open (about 6 to 8 minutes). Discard any mussels that remain closed.

Remove the mussels from liquid. Strain liquid through a dampened cloth and measure it. Add fish broth to make 4 cups. Return liquid to the kettle (rinsed to remove any sand).

Remove the mussels from shells, discarding shells. Pinch out and discard any "beards" from the mussels.

To the liquid add the cream. Bring to a boil over high heat, reduce heat slightly, and boil until soup is reduced by about one-fourth. Lower heat to medium. Taste, and add salt if needed. Add the mussels and cook just until heated through. Serve hot or chilled, garnished with parsley.   SERVES: 6

THE KITCHEN TABLE IN THE HOUSE where I grew up on Divinity Street in Philadelphia seemed to represent the exact center of the Curry universe. It was at that table that ordinary meals—breakfast, lunch, and dinner—were served daily. The dining room was reserved for special Sunday-night dinners, Thanksgiving, Christmas, or particularly when we had guests. But it was that oblong, light-blond kitchen table that seemed to witness the entire ebb and flow of our lives. It was at that table that my father first gave me permission to get my driver's license when I turned sixteen. It was at that table that I learned that my sister-in-law was pregnant. It was also at that table that we had quite a family scene when my sister announced that she was leaving for the convent. I wondered, as I myself made the announcement that I wanted to leave for the Jesuits . . . what would replace that kitchen table? What would replace that instrument by which our daily lives were touched?

When I entered the Society of Jesus in 1961 there was a rather formal afternoon snack known as afternoon *haustus,* a Latin word. According to the common rule, haustus was always to be eaten standing and in silence. After we had been outside, either playing or working for the afternoon, we would trudge up the back stairs of the scullery in our work clothing. There we would stand around a large, three-tiered trolley called a *plaustrum,* on which would be served vast amounts of leftover corn bread, rolls, vats of peanut butter and jelly, ice-cold milk, hot chocolate, or, in the summertime, iced tea and lemonade. It was amazing, the amount of food that young men could consume after a workout on the handball court or in the fields. As our lives, not to mention ourselves, matured in the Society of Jesus, the scullery was replaced with what we would call a coffee room or a haustus room in many of our communities.

To me, a community's haustus room reveals just how warm and friendly that community is going to be. Some coffee rooms are rather spartan, and one is lucky to find even a pot of brewing coffee. Sometimes, you have to look behind every cabinet door to find sugar, or milk, or tea. Other haustus rooms are quite generous and lavish in their accoutrements. Georgetown University's haustus room is not only stocked full of wonderful things to eat and drink, but is also spacious, very bright and colorful, and notably clean. Actually, the schedule of the men at Georgetown is so hectic that you could go into the haustus room at almost any time and get a half-decent meal out of the refrigerators. But more than the canned soups or the coffee or tea that is made available to the community it's the conversation, and the badinage—that exchange between men who are very busy, but very happy to see you, even if it's just for the space of one cup of coffee—where the warmth of that particular community is revealed. Haustus provides us a space to breathe, to find out how the day is going, what the evening holds, or what the morning produced. It's the way a family unconsciously lets each other know what they are up to, and about. I have always found that the haustus room is really the strongest part of a religious community, far less self-conscious than the chapel, even less self-conscious than the community recreation room. It is in those unguarded moments that one really finds out what it means to live as a brother in Christ.

Vegetable Soup

1 veal shin, the bone sawed into three pieces and cracked (about 2
*   pounds)*
8 cups water
Bouquet garni of:
*   ½ onion*
*   1 clove garlic*
*   1 sprig of thyme*
*   1 sprig of chervil*
*   4 sprigs of parsley*
*   3 basil leaves*
*   2 green onions, with tops, cut up*
*   1 bay leaf*
Kernels cut from 3 ears of corn
¼ pound okra, rinsed, trimmed, and cut in ½-inch pieces
2 medium potatoes, peeled and coarsely chopped
2 large ripe tomatoes

IN A SOUP KETTLE, combine the veal shin, the water, and the
bouquet garni. Bring the water to a boil, reduce the heat, and simmer
the veal bones, covered, skimming as necessary, for 1 hour. Discard
the bouquet garni.

To the contents of the kettle, add the corn, okra, potatoes,
and tomatoes. Continue simmering the mixture for 1 hour. Strain the
broth and reserve it. Discard the veal bones. In the container of a food
processor or blender, puree the vegetables; return the puree to the
broth.

SERVES: 6

The funeral services are conducted either in the chapel or in the church, with the brothers acting as pallbearers.

WE LIVE OUR LIFE in common as Jesuits, and so, of course, we die in common. When a member of our order dies, the superior first goes into the deceased brother's room to retrieve personal effects that the man's family might want to have. However, the rest of the man's clothing, and some other items—since our clothing is all in common—are listed on a blackboard, so that brothers with worn gear might get replacements. We're not talking about some Filene's basement mob scene here, or the old crones in *Zorba,* but clothes do wear out, and, as I say, we all wear the same things in common.

I needed a watch at one time, and so I went in, as we had to do, and asked my superior for permission to acquire a watch. "Oh, fine, sure," he said, going to a drawer, quickly rifling it and drawing forth Father Hunter Guthrie's watch. "Nice watch," I said, slipping it on my wrist. It fit perfectly. I went home soon after, and over the soup course, my father noticed the timepiece peeking out from my cuff. "Nice watch," Dad says, "where'd you get it?" "Oh, it was Father Guthrie's watch." "You're wearing a dead priest's watch?" he said, shaking his head. "I don't believe it." Then his eyes drifted down to my shiny black shoes. "No, Dad," I said, "I bought these myself, but you should have seen the nice pair Brother Alvey just picked up from Father Lenny."

Bell Pepper Soup

2 cups finely minced bell pepper

1 cup minced onion

¼ cup minced carrot

1 clove garlic, minced

3 slices bacon, minced

2 cups peeled and chopped ripe tomatoes

4 cups beef and/or chicken stock

½ teaspoon salt

¼ teaspoon black pepper

½ teaspoon minced fresh basil

1 pound ground round steak

SAUTÉ THE BELL PEPPER, onion, carrot, garlic, and bacon together, until the bacon is slightly browned. Add the rest of the ingredients, including the steak. Cover and bring to a boil, then lower the heat and simmer for 45 minutes. Adjust seasonings to taste.

SERVES: 6

Index

A

Accolti, Father, 178
Advent, 10, 15–58
America, 60, 123
America House, 197
Amos, 88–89
Amsterdam, 188
Anderson, George, 60
apple and chicken soup, cream
    of, 187
Arrupe, Father Pedro, 43
asparagus soup, 170
attention to duty, 123–24
avocado soup, 180

B

Baddit, Mr., 86
bakery, 101–5
Banderas, Brother, 43
bank accounts, 131–32
barbers, 45
baseball, 126–27
basket making, 153–55
bean(s):
    black, sherried soup, 96–97
    chickpea and vegetable soup,
        143
    green, and ham soup, 78
    lima, soup, 145

minestrone Milanese,
    114–15
soup, Brazilian black, 196
soup, Spanish, 23–24
white, and smoked pork
    soup, 106
bean sprout soup, 130
beef:
    borscht, 46
    Hungarian goulash, 40
    meatballs, 134
    minestrone Milanese,
        114–15
    pot-au-feu, 28
    stock, 11, 13
Bellarmine, St. Robert, 20
Berlin, 98
Bernard, Sister, 52–54
Biniakiewicz, Brother, 136
black bean soup:
    Brazilian, 196
    sherried, 96–97
Blaszczak, Jerry, 174–75
blindness, 81–82, 101, 194
Bloomfield, Morris and Esther,
    110
boat making, 155–56, 164
Boller, Father Ken, 6
bongo bongo soup, 76
Borgia, St. Francis, 22
borscht, 46
Brazilian black bean soup, 196
bread dumplings, 83
breads, 4–5, 101–2

Brendan, St., 164
broccoli:
    peasant soup, 122
    and potato soup, Irish, 58
brown stock, 14
Bruelman, Herman, 98–99

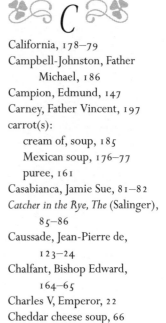

C

California, 178–79
Campbell-Johnston, Father
    Michael, 186
Campion, Edmund, 147
Carney, Father Vincent, 197
carrot(s):
    cream of, soup, 185
    Mexican soup, 176–77
    puree, 161
Casabianca, Jamie Sue, 81–82
Catcher in the Rye, The (Salinger),
    85–86
Caussade, Jean-Pierre de,
    123–24
Chalfant, Bishop Edward,
    164–65
Charles V, Emperor, 22
Cheddar cheese soup, 66
cheerleading, 144
chicken:
    and apple soup, cream of,
        187
    balls, 36

chicken (*cont.*)
bean sprout soup, 130
leg noodle soup, 80
meat stock, 13
soup, 18, 19
soup, glorified cream of, 87
stock, 11–13
zuppa maritata, 35
chickpea and vegetable soup, 143
china, 141–42
chowder:
clam, 157
corn, 159
crab, 158
dried corn, 69
Christmas, 10, 59–108
Church of St. Francis Xavier, 188–89
clam:
chowder, 157
and mushroom soup, 71
Claver, Peter, 25
clear tomato soup, 21
Collins, Dominic, 57
communities, 169
Company, 186
Considine, Robert, 53
Convent of Divine Love, 166–67
corn:
chowder, 159
cream of, soup, 33
dried, chowder, 69
vegetable soup, 202
crab:
chowder, 158
lobster bisque, 192
cream:
of carrot soup, 185
of chicken and apple soup, 187
of chicken soup, glorified, 87
of corn soup, 33
of fresh tomato soup, 48

lobster bisque, 192
of mushroom soup, French, 94
mussel soup billy-bi, 198
potage Saint-Cloud, 173
vichyssoise, 152
Creole soup, Peruvian, 42
Curry, Denise, 47, 74, 107, 126–27, 129, 166, 199
Curry, Jack, 129

Daly, Reverend Leo, 50
Davis, Father Thurston, 47
death, 203
De Smet, Father, 178
difference and individuality, 169
dill pickle soup, 137
disabilities, 62, 193–95
bakery and, 101–5
blindness, 81–82, 101, 194
National Theatre Workshop of the Handicapped (NTWH) and, 49–50, 95, 102–5, 146, 153, 171, 172, 181, 193
reporter and, 102–5
Dixon, Brother Frank, 79
Dolan, James, 60–61
Dominican Academy, 41
Donohue, Father John W., 60, 123–24
Dougherty, Father Frank, 85–86
dried corn chowder, 69
dumplings, bread, 83

Easter, 10, 111, 112, 163–204
eggplant soup, 183

elderly, 65
England, Owen's work in, 146–49
equipment, 9–10
escarole soup, 133
Esquivel, Laura, 95, 175
Eziguera, Brother, 4–5

Faber, Father Peter, 22, 25
fans, 79
fasting, 112, 116
Flora, Sister Jo Anne, 107
France, 120–21
Francis de Sales, St., 169
French:
cream of mushroom soup, 94
onion soup, 100
vegetable soup, 125

Garate, Brother Francis, 43
Gardner, Ann, 171, 172
garlic soup, 44
Garnet, Father, 146, 147–48
Georgetown University, 200
Germany, 98–99
glorified cream of chicken soup, 87
Golden Jubilees, 65, 186
golden squash soup, 107–8
goulash, Hungarian, 40
Goupil, St. René, 27
Gray, Peter, 126
green bean and ham soup, 78
Guthrie, Father Hunter, 203

H

haircuts, 45
"Hallelujah Chorus," 67–68
ham:
    and green bean soup, 78
    lentil, and vegetable soup,
        Swiss, 55–56
    Spanish bean soup, 23–24
haustus, 199–201
Havas, John, 60–61
Hawley, John, 70
Haystack School of Crafts,
    154–55
Helsinger, Rich, 155
hiding places, 146–49
historian, 184
Holy Week in Mexico, 174–75
homelessness, 47
Hungarian goulash, 40

I

ice truck, 88–89
Ignatius Loyola, St., 6–7, 8, 15,
    22, 25, 38, 59, 109, 111,
    116, 124, 151
Internet, 186
Ireland, 57
Irish potato and broccoli soup,
    58
Isabella, Empress, 22
Italy, 181–82

J

Jesuit brotherhood, 38–39
Jogues, St. Isaac, 27, 31
Jogues Bowl, 31
John Paul II, Pope, 135

K

kale and potato soup, 64
Katie, Aunt, 52–54
Kieren, Sister Helen, 41
kitchen, 8–9
kitchen table, 199
kneeling, 151
Koch, Ed, 34
Kostka, Stanislaus, 135

L

Lacey, Joe, 144
Lavin, Father Henry, 29
leeks:
    carrot puree, 161
    vichyssoise, 152
Lent, 10, 109–61
lentil, ham, and vegetable soup,
    Swiss, 55–56
Life of Little Margaret, The, 43,
    181–82
light-up, 3–4
Like Water for Chocolate
    (Esquivel), 95, 175
lima bean soup, 145
Linehan, Dennis Michael, 120
lobster bisque, 192
LoRe, Louis, 181
Loyola Castle, 4

M

McGuire, John, 154
McShay, Bishop Joseph, 91
Madrid, 62–63
Majsa, Janice, 39
Manifestation of Conscience,
    146

Margaret of Costello, 181–82
Martin, James, 60
matzo balls, 84
Mayer, Herbert, 171, 172
meat:
    borscht, 46
    green bean and ham soup, 78
    Hungarian goulash, 40
    minestrone Milanese,
        114–15
    Peruvian Creole soup, 42
    pot-au-feu, 28
    Spanish bean soup, 23–24
    stocks, 11, 12, 13–14
    Swiss lentil, ham, and
        vegetable soup, 55–56
    white bean and smoked pork
        soup, 106
meatballs, 134
    escarole soup, 133
Mexican soup, 176–77
Mexico, 174–75
minestrone Milanese, 114–15
Moore, Kirk, 9
Mother Teresa, 34
mushroom:
    and clam soup, 71
    potato soup, 90
    soup, French cream of, 94
    and tomato soup, 128
mussel soup billy-bi, 198

N

Nadal, Father Jeronimo, 7
National Public Radio, 102
National Theatre Workshop of
    the Handicapped
    (NTWH), 49–50, 95,
    102–5, 146, 153, 171,
    172, 181, 193
New York Health and Racquet
    Club, 197

Nobili, Father, 178
noodle soup, chicken leg, 80
North American martyrs, 27,
31

O

O'Hare, Father Joseph, 197
onion(s):
    Mexican soup, 176–77
    soup, French, 100
    soupe de compiègne, 30
orange and tomato soup, 190
Owen, Brother Nicholas ("Little
    John"), 146–49
oyster(s):
    bongo bongo soup, 76
    stew, 72

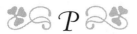

P

patience, 17
peasant soup, 122
penance, 138–39, 151
pepper, bell:
    Mexican soup, 176–77
    red, soup, 51
    soup, 204
Peruvian Creole soup, 42
Philip Neri, Sister, 73, 91, 92,
    93
piano lessons, 91, 92, 93
pickle soup, dill, 137
Pink Sisters (Convent of
    Divine Love),
    166–67
Pius V, Pope, 22
pork:
    meatballs, 134
    Peruvian Creole soup,
        42

smoked, and white bean
    soup, 106
    see also ham
potage aux fines herbes, 168
potage Saint-Cloud, 173
potato(es):
    and broccoli soup, Irish, 58
    and kale soup, 64
    mushroom soup, 90
    soup, base for, 14
    vegetable soup, 202
    vichyssoise, 152
pot-au-feu, 28
pots, 10, 18
poultry:
    bean sprout soup, 130
    chicken balls, 36
    chicken leg noodle soup, 80
    chicken soup, 18, 19
    chicken stock, 11–13
    cream of chicken and apple
        soup, 187
    glorified cream of chicken
        soup, 87
    in meat stock, 13
    zuppa maritata, 35
prayer, 7, 8, 117–18
Psalm 25, 16
Psalm 27, 17
Puccia, Lucia, 181

R

red bell pepper soup, 51
Redington, Father Jimmy,
    88–89
Reilly, Brother, 77
Rodriguez, St. Alphonsus, 25,
    43, 188–89
Rome, 43
Royal Board on Education and
    Care of Handicapped
    Persons, 62

S

St. Aloysius Gonzaga Grammar
    School, 52–54
St. Francis De Sales, 91
St. Isaac Jogues (Wernersville,
    Pa.), 5, 20, 31–32,
    67–68, 116, 141
St. John's Hain's Lutheran
    Church, 67–68
St. Joseph's Prep, 85, 144
St. Joseph's University, 29,
    113
St. Lucy's Blind School,
    91–92
St. Peter's Cathedral, 135
St. Vincent Ferrer, 171–72
Salinger, J. D., 85
seafood:
    bongo bongo soup, 76
    clam and mushroom soup,
        71
    clam chowder, 157
    crab chowder, 158
    lobster bisque, 192
    mussel soup billy-bi, 198
    oyster stew, 72
Secrets of Jesuit Breadmaking, The
    (Curry), 4, 37, 70, 102,
    174
Sheffler, Shelly, 49–50
sherried black bean soup,
    96–97
Sofia, Queen, 62
soupe de compiègne, 30
soups, 4–5, 7–8, 10–11
Spain, 62–63
Spanish bean soup, 23–24
spinach:
    bongo bongo soup, 76
    soup, 150
    Spanish bean soup,
        23–24
spiritual adviser, 184

squash soup:
    golden, 107–8
    winter, 119
    zucchini, 140
stew, oyster, 72
stock, 10–14
    beef, 11, 13
    beginning, 12–13
    brown, 14
    chicken, 11–13
    clarifying, 13
    meat, 11, 12, 13–14
    vegetable, 11, 14
Stokes, Father Tom, 65
superior, sheltering of, 191
sweet potato soup, 26
Swiss lentil, ham, and vegetable
    soup, 55–56

tap dancing lessons, 92
television shows, early-
    morning, 37–38
Thanksgiving, 31–32
tomato(es):
    cream of fresh, soup, 48
    Mexican soup, 176–77

minestrone Milanese,
    114–15
and mushroom soup,
    128
and orange soup, 190
soup, 21
vegetable soup, 202
tools, 9–10

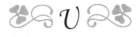

utensils, 9–10

Van Ban Schoten, Steven, 93
Vaux, Ann, 146
vegetable(s):
    and chickpea soup, 143
    lentil, and ham soup, Swiss,
        55–56
    soup, 202
    soup, French, 125
    stock, 11, 14
vichyssoise, 152
Villa days, 116–18

waiting, 16–17
Wernersville, Pa., St. Isaac
    Jogues in, 5, 20, 31–32,
    67–68, 116, 141
West Reading Art Museum,
    117
White, Joel, 155
white bean and smoked pork
    soup, 106
winter squash soup, 119
wisdom, 86
Wooden Boat School, 155–56,
    164
work space, 9

Xavier, St. Francis, 73–75

zucchini soup, 140
zuppa maritata, 35